GRANDKIDS Camp

A Handbook for Leaving a Legacy Through Unforgettable Experiences Rooted in God's Word

Linda Quinones

For more information, grandkidscampQ@gmail.com

First paperback edition April 2026

ISBN 979-8-218-88006-4

Library of Congress Control Number: 2026903897

To my grandmother Nancy Shively (1919-2026).

Her legacy is one of grace and faith, a beautiful example of family love that spanned over a century.

To my parents, Dave and Ann Hilyard who have been an example to me of intentional grandparenting.

I am grateful for the hours of prayer and words of encouragement you have spoken into my life and into the lives of my children, and now my grandchildren over the years.

To my husband, Neal, my best friend for over 40 years.

Your support and partnership make Grandkids Camp possible—and turn it into one of our greatest shared joys.

And for our children and grandchildren.

I pray you will use God's word to continue the Christian legacy of our family.

Contents

Introduction

And Jesus came and said to them, "All authority in heaven and on earth has been given to me. Go therefore and make disciples of all nations, baptizing them in the name of the Father and of the Son and of the Holy Spirit, teaching them to observe all that I have commanded you. And behold, I am with you always, to the end of the age." Matthew 28:18-20

All it took was one magazine article to inspire and impact children for generations to come.

Sometimes, it takes just that one simple idea—one article, one spark—to change the course of a family for generations. For us, that spark came from the pages of Focus on the Family magazine, through a short feature about intentional grandparenting—specifically, hosting a camp for their grandkids—that stirred something deep within my parents' hearts. They had no idea that their response to that inspiration would one day ripple through our family, shaping faith, memories, and relationships that would last.

Today's children face challenges unlike any generation before them. The pressures of modern life seem to find them earlier and earlier—broken families, the cruelty of bullying, and the endless noise of technology that competes for their attention and interferes with normal child development. It's no wonder that many children drift away from many things that could be good for them and truly matter, especially that of a relationship with God. Knowing this is the world we live in, our family made a choice—a commitment—to live out the words of Jesus in Matthew 28:18–20, to be intentional grandparents who guide our children and grandchildren, toward Christ. Faith isn't something we simply hope they'll stumble into: it's something we pray for, model, nurture, and weave into our time together.

That's how "Grandkids Camp" was born.

After reading that article, my parents first began a "Grandkids Camp" to create something special for their grandchildren, similar to the concept in the *Focus on the Family Magazine*. For those who don't know, Grandkids Camp is where my parents (and later my husband and I) invited all their grandchildren at the time for 2-5 days in order to have fun, make memories, and share God's Word with them, not to mention to give their parents a little break.

Eventually, my husband and I joined in, continuing the tradition they began, using each camp to intentionally plant seeds for the next generation of disciples among the memories and fun. We plan carefully to find a time when all the grandchildren can attend, as it is more meaningful when they can all be together. Every year has its own theme with a Bible verse to memorize, and thoughtfully designed Bible stories related to the theme, along with corresponding activities, crafts, and sometimes even the snacks reinforce the theme. The children come expecting swimming and s'mores, but they leave with something far deeper: memories of being loved, seen, and guided by grandparents who care as much about their souls as their smiles.

It reminded us that sometimes, God plants extraordinary seeds in the most ordinary places—like the pages of a magazine left open on a kitchen table—and when watered with love and intention, they can grow into something that blesses generations.

This book is one tool to help you become intentional grandparents, leaving a legacy for the next generation. You may choose to host a Grandkids Camp for a week, a few days, or a few hours. Whichever way you choose to use the ideas in this book, cover them in prayer to make those times meaningful as you point your grandchildren to Jesus.

The Origins of Grandkids Camp

The inaugural Grandkids Camp, hosted by my parents, took place in 2001 while they were living in Georgia. Over the course of six years, they organized three Grandkids Camps. Each year, they alternated between Grandkids Camp and an extended family vacation, making sure our time together was both memorable and spiritually meaningful.

My mom, known as Mammaw to my kids and their cousins, wanted to start Grandkids Camp because she and my dad lived quite far from all their grandchildren, so she was looking for a way to spend quality time with them beyond the brief visits during holidays or family gatherings. Her goal for Grandkids Camp was to foster deeper relationships with her grandkids, allowing everyone to get to know each other better. Of course, they also aimed to have a lot of fun together.

For the first Grandkids Camp, they chose Hershey Campground in Pennsylvania because it was convenient for all their children to bring the grandkids. They booked a full week at the campground with their small camper and decided to host one family of grandchildren at a time. From there, they welcomed 2 groups of 3 children for 2 1/2 days each, followed by a group of 4 children for the remaining 2 1/2 days. The week ended with all the parents arriving at camp together for the July 4th holiday. Despite the rustic camping conditions, the grandchildren loved fishing, hiking, crafts, and simply spending uninterrupted time with Poppop and Mammaw.

The second Grandkids Camp was again held at Hershey Campground, but this time they brought all ten of their grandchildren together, renting two campers on separate campsites, which weren't exactly close to each other. My dad, Poppop, stayed in the camper with four grandsons, while Mammaw stayed in the camper with the six granddaughters. Even though the campsites were a bit far apart, all their meals and activities were shared together. The children cherished the opportunity to play with cousins, swimming, doing crafts, and deepening their bond with their grandparents.

By 2005, the grandchildren were older, and my parents were living on the quiet summer campus of Toccoa Falls College in Georgia. They hosted their final Grandkids Camp at the college using an unused student house (for the older children)—later affectionately nicknamed the "condemned house," since it was torn down the following year; the younger children stayed in my parents' small house. Staying in the house with their cousins was a huge highlight (for the older children.)

Poppop and Mammaw found that year to be the most enjoyable for several reasons. The grandchildren were older, which made everything easier, and they could participate in more complex games, activities, and events—like horseback riding and the ropes course.

This ended up being the last time all the grandkids stayed together. Soon after, Poppop and Mammaw moved from Georgia to Pennsylvania, and with the oldest grandchild turning seventeen, the logistics of hosting all the grandchildren became too challenging, and the tradition shifted to smaller gatherings or one-on-one visits.

During the years when Grandkids Camp wasn't happening, my parents adjusted by spending more one-on-one time with individual grandkids or small groups of two to three at a time. My daughter, the oldest grandchild, had a memorable solo visit with her grandparents—it was also her first time flying alone from Maryland to Georgia; she really cherished that personal attention. The other grandkids who visited with cousins also enjoyed special moments, not only with their grandparents but also with the cousin closest in age.

We, my husband and I, have decided to carry on the tradition by hosting a Grandkids Camp of our own. We have four children—three of whom are married—and eight grandchildren as of 2026. During a family gathering, we introduced the idea of holding a Grandkids Camp for our grandchildren. Our adult children were thrilled, eagerly reminiscing about the fun they had at Grandkids Camps when they were younger. They even joked about the possibility of Poppop and Mammaw (then 80 and 76) hosting another camp for them as adults. When I shared this with my parents, they laughed at the idea but were clearly delighted to know that the tradition is still so cherished by their grandchildren.

I am passionate about the idea of Grandkids Camp because I see it as a special way to invest in my grandchildren's lives, just as my parents did. I'm deeply grateful that my grandchildren are being raised by Christian parents who are committed to teaching them according to God's Word. My goal isn't to take the place of their parents, but to be an additional source of guidance and encouragement through this camp.

Grandkids Camp is about far more than simply creating fun memories. It's an intentional opportunity to share the gospel and to help my grandchildren understand that real patience, gratitude, and obedience are possible only through a relationship with Jesus. I want them to know that apart from Him, we cannot truly live out these lessons. It is through submitting to Jesus that we receive the power of the Holy Spirit, who enables us to live in ways that please God.

Ultimately, my hope is that the lessons and values we share at camp will stay with our grandchildren—shaping their faith and character long after the camp ends, just as my parents' example shaped the lives of their own grandchildren.

We've been fortunate to have a vacation home by a lake, which has become the perfect location for our Grandkids Camp. This setting not only provides a wonderful environment for making memories but also fits with our purpose of using our resources for the glory of God. Like my parents' choice of campground or college campus, the location is secondary to the purpose: quality time spent loving, teaching, and making disciples of the next generation.

I first began thinking about writing this book after we hosted our inaugural Grandkids Camp in 2018. When I started sharing our experiences and ideas on social media, the response was overwhelming—people wanted to know more, and their curiosity planted the seed for what has now become this book.

In 2020, my husband and I read *Life Mastery* by Bob Shank, where he emphasized the importance of crafting a life purpose statement. Together, we wrote ours:

"Our purpose in life is to pursue God through His Word, to make disciples, serve others, give generously to the making of disciples, and use all our resources for the glory of God."

We want this statement to reflect the Great Commission in Matthew 28, and writing this book feels like a natural extension of that purpose. Our desire is not only to disciple our grandchildren but also to encourage and equip you, as the grandparent and/or parent, to do the same with your own children and grandchildren.

My hope is that this book will inspire my grandchildren to one day look back with fondness on the fun they had, the lessons they learned, and the faith they witnessed during our Grandkids Camps. And perhaps, when their time comes, they will carry on the tradition—maybe even at our lake house—with their own grandchildren.

Our Family Spiritual History

Although my parents didn't originally set up Grandkids Camp with a spiritual focus, they made sure to include daily devotions each morning. Their goal was to influence their grandchildren's faith in Jesus through these shared moments. Their deep love for the Lord and the way they lived out their faith has had a profound impact on all their grandchildren, both spiritually and non-spiritually.

Our Grandkids Camp is centered on sharing the good news of Jesus with our grandchildren through daily activities and meaningful time together, faith has been deeply rooted in our heritage. For generations, a relationship with God—and the special bond between grandparents and grandchildren—has been a vital part of our family life. My husband and I are both at least third-generation Christians, and we're committed to continuing that legacy in our own family.

My dad didn't have much of a relationship with his own grandparents. As the fifth of eight children, he later said, "My grandparents were old" by the time he was born; that experience motivated him to build strong bonds with his grandchildren and strengthen connections among cousins.

Dad was not the first Christian in our family. His parents, Grandma and Grandpa Hilyard, weren't believers in Jesus when they married but came to faith after their first two children were born. Poppop grew up with devoted parents and a strong Sunday school foundation, committing his life to Jesus at 12, and was baptized at 13.

My mom was raised in a Christian home and grew up deeply rooted in the life of the church. Her mother—my Grandma Cornman Shively—was consistently involved in church activities even as a child and was baptized between the ages of 10 and 12, once she was old enough to truly understand the gospel.

Faith ran deep in the generations before her, as my mom's grandparents left a lasting spiritual legacy. Her grandfather, once skeptical of Jesus and the Bible, came to faith after witnessing a miraculous event within the family when he was older in life. Her grandmother, raised in a Christian home, devoted herself to the church, teaching Sunday school and living out her faith with quiet dedication.

At fourteen, my mom repented of her sins and surrendered her life to Jesus during an evangelistic meeting; that moment marked the beginning of a lifelong hunger for God's Word and a steadfast walk of faith.

On my husband Neal's side, we also inherit a rich spiritual heritage. Neal came to the United States from the Philippines when he was seven years old. His parents, whom our children call *Lolo* and *Lola* (Tagalog for grandfather and grandmother), embraced and nurtured their faith, rededicating their lives to Christ after marriage and raising a spiritually grounded family. Neal's grandparents, *Nanay* and *Tatay* (Tagalog for mom and dad), came to faith through the persistent outreach of a church group from Manila that visited their home every Sunday to share the gospel. After many years of faithful visits, Nanay and Tatay surrendered their lives to the Lord, and the entire family was baptized together at the church. They grew in their faith and helped plant churches in the Philippines and later in Southern California, once they moved to the States.

As you can see, both sides of our family have experienced the glory of God in their lives and have shared a deep desire to see their children walk in the footsteps of Jesus. This heritage of faith is part of my inspiration for Grandkids Camp. We are blessed with an amazing spiritual heritage, and through Grandkids Camp, we hope to continue that legacy for generations to come. Even if you don't have a similar spiritual heritage, it can begin with you.

So far, we have hosted seven Grandkids Camps, with grandchildren ranging in age from 2 to 10 years old—sometimes as many as 6 at a time! Each year included a new theme, complete with Bible stories, memory verses, and plenty of fun crafts and activities to help them remember the theme. We've watched our grandchildren form lasting friendships with their cousins, and it warms our hearts to hear them excitedly recall what they learned. One grandchild even described Grandkids Camp as "a highlight of my summer."

To help you create your own Grandkids Camp, what follows are the weekly lessons that I created for Grandkids Camp, according to the theme of the year. I have thought through each lesson with the question, "How can this truth lead my grandchildren to the cross?" These lessons and activities have grown out of our own experiences, and we pray they inspire meaningful connections, joyful memories, and a lifelong love for God in your family as well.

In the chapters ahead, you'll find detailed plans for each year's theme—resources designed to equip and inspire you to host your own Grandkids Camp and pass on a spiritual legacy that will stay with your grandchildren for a lifetime.

Before we move on to the lessons, we need to start with some basic instructions so you have everything you need to set up your Grandkids Camp in advance.

My Notes

Basics

The lessons, crafts, and activities in this book are designed for grandchildren ages two to twelve. Some projects may need to be adapted depending on a child's age, and suggestions for modification are provided throughout.

This guide is structured around a four-day camp schedule, offering four days of Bible lessons paired with engaging activities. You are welcome to follow the plan in its entirety or select the portions that best meet your needs.

Set up

As you have read in the introduction chapter, I organize each Grandkids Camp with a variety of fun activities, delicious food, engaging crafts, and meaningful Bible lessons, centered around a specific Bible verse for the kids to memorize. Even a two-year-old can master a Bible verse in just a few days of repeating it, so I never underestimated their ability to remember.

I spend a lot of time researching stories, activities, fun foods, and crafts that align with the chosen theme each year. This book shares those themes, along with all the details of what I did to help you plan and run your own Grandkids Camp.

Before the camp, I print the Bible verse in large print and hang it near the rules for the camp, placing both close to the table where we do activities and have meals; that way, we can review the verse and the rules throughout the day. We also make sure to keep the parents involved by sharing the week's theme, the Bible verse, and the ways we were helping their children apply it. At the end of the week, we record the children reciting the week's Bible verses, which we send to their parents as a keepsake and is one of my favorite moments of the camp. It is incredible to see how well they remember the verse—and to witness their joy and confidence as they share it on video.

Suggested Resources

We read the Bible stories from the following resources. Please feel free to use these or your favorite version of the Bible.

- *The Message Bible*
- *The Jesus Storybook Bible*
- *The Beginners Bible*

Invitations

To officially start the camp, I love sending out special invitations to the grandkids for Grandkids Camp—there's just something magical about a child receiving something in the mail addressed just to them. (Readers, I've included some sample invitations in the appendix for easy reference and inspiration for your own camps.)

One of our more creative ideas for invitations came from a trip to the craft store, where we picked up some customizable puzzles. PaQ (the grandkids' name for my husband Neal) would write the invitation message directly on the puzzle, and then we'd take it apart and mail the pieces to the grandkids. They had to put the puzzle together to discover the invitation, adding an element of surprise and making the experience even more memorable for all.

Another year, I bought a helium balloon, attached the invitation to the end of the string, and personally delivered it to the local grandchildren. Our grand-godson, however, was living in another state at the time, so for him, I tied the invitation to a helium balloon, placed it in a large box, wrapped it up, and mailed it to him. I warned his mom to avoid using a sharp object to open the box. When he opened the box, the balloon floated up with the invitation tied to the string. He was overjoyed to receive the package, and his mom sent us a video of him seeing the balloon float out of the box as he opened it. He then wrote a big "Yes" on the back of the invitation and sent us a picture to confirm his excitement about coming.

One year, I included a list of possible activities for the camp with the invitation and asked the kids to circle their favorites. Most of the activities were familiar, such as swimming, crafts, baking cookies, eating ice cream, etc., but I wanted to find out which activities they truly loved and would want to repeat for that year's Grandkids Camp. It was a simple way to involve them in the camp planning and get them even more excited about what was coming.

Rules

We establish a set of camp rules for the house, with the first and most popular being NO PARENTS. To attend, children need to be at least two years old and potty-trained by three, though we make exceptions as needed.

Here are some of the other rules we set:

- No Parents
- Obey MaQ and PaQ.
- Don't go down to the dock without an adult.
- Clean up your toys after you finish playing with them.
- Must be potty-trained by age three in order to attend (we sometimes make exceptions to this rule).

- No complaining–be grateful (this was based on our first Grandkids Camp theme, but we kept it for future camps as a reminder).
- Say please and thank you.
- Love one another.
- Have fun!!

I post the rules prominently so they can be easily referenced whenever needed, especially when the kids aren't following them.

Schedule

As someone who thrives on organization, I put together a tentative schedule for each day of Grandkids Camp, basing on the kids' usual routines at home—when they woke up, napped, and went to bed. Below is a sample schedule I used, especially during the early years. I include meals and snacks to help the day flow smoothly from one activity to the next.

While I found having a set schedule incredibly helpful, I also made sure to build in plenty of flexibility. If a strict schedule isn't your style, you might prefer simply making a list of activities and choosing based on the children's mood and energy that day. This sample schedule is just a starting point—you can easily adjust this template to fit your own approach and needs.

Daily schedule sample

Breakfast
Introduce Theme, Rules,
Bible verse (practice 2-3 times)
Theme song (if you have one)
Bible lesson
Activity/Game/Object lesson/Craft
Snack
Outdoor play–swim, fish, etc.
Lunch

Naps
Afternoon boat ride or walk in the woods
Dinner
Baths
Evening activity/story
Bedtime
Record the children reciting their verse (for last day)

Since we frequent this location for our camp often, the lake house, I'm familiar with the many activities available nearby we can do. Our outdoor play usually includes water-based fun like swimming, fishing, boating, kayaking, and feeding the fish or ducks at the nearby marina, where the large carp are always eager for a meal. In the afternoons, we often enjoy similar activities but sometimes add a boat ride for ice cream, miniature golf, or a scavenger hunt in the woods. The nearby state park has a beach area the kids love, along with woodland trails. As they've grown older, we've planned to explore other options of fun like gold-panning and educational programs at the park. We're also close to an amusement park, which we've visited for a day trip once the kids were past their nap stage.

When the children were younger, they usually took an afternoon nap, which provided a much-needed break for my husband and me. As they get older, this time shifts to quiet reading or offers a rare chance for games or puzzles that require more time. We make an effort to limit both TV and electronic use during camp time so there is more time for the other activities.

For after-dinner activities, we aimed to help everyone wind down with relaxing options like reading or movie nights. One highlight is our annual bonfire, where we roast marshmallows and make s'mores. Although we only have the bonfire one night each year, due to the impact of too many marshmallows on the sleep patterns of younger kids, it remains a much-anticipated event. Additionally, we've introduced our grandkids to hide and seek inside the house, which has become a beloved evening game.

Meals

I plan meals in advance, buying food based on preferences shared by their parents. From there, I create a menu that balances their favorites with some new options, keeping lunch and dinner simple and healthy. By repeating similar menus each year, I am able to minimize prep time while still offering nutritious choices for everyone. For more complex dishes, I invite interested kids to help with manageable tasks, encouraging their involvement, and giving them a sense of contribution. Even if a meal isn't their favorite, they usually eat well—especially with the promise of dessert. PaQ often uses this option to his advantage, revealing tempting treats we have for dessert or offering a small taste to motivate them to finish their meals. We also make sure to stock up on savory snacks, like cheesy popcorn, for our grandchild who prefers those over sweet desserts.

Sample meals

Breakfast: Cereal, eggs, toast, or pancakes and fruit

Lunch: Grilled cheese and carrots, macaroni and cheese with hot dogs, peanut butter and jelly sandwich, and fruit

Dinner: Grilled chicken with rice and fried zucchini, hamburgers with tater tots, fish sticks with rice and green beans

Snacks don't always follow the theme, but whenever possible, I try to connect them to our annual theme or the story of the day. Often, I choose snacks based on what I know the kids enjoy or what would be fun to make together. One memorable treat was "dirt and worms." I told the kids we were going to eat dirt and worms as a snack. Once they saw that the snack was actually a combination of pudding, crushed Oreos and gummy worms, they loved it. You can find the recipe for dirt and worms in the Recipe Appendix.

Supplies

Disposable tablecloths from the dollar store to protect the workspace are ideal for activities at Grandkids Camp. You can easily roll up the mess and throw it away once a project is completed.

Old T-shirt or smocks are helpful to protect clothing for painting and other messy activities. For each day of the camp, I prepare a bin or box with all the craft supplies in one place and label them Day 1, Day 2, etc.

To ensure everyone gets their crafts back at the end of the camp, I place each child's creations into a bag labeled with their name. During craft activities, I encourage the kids to write their names on their work, or if they are not yet able to write, we help to add their name to their craft. This way, each child feels proud of their work and knows which ones belong to them.

Keys to success

The most important key to success is covering your Grandkids Camp with prayer. Prayer invites God into every step of the process—from planning and preparation to each moment spent together. Pray as you plan and prepare, pray throughout Grandkids Camp, and continue praying after it is over, asking God to plant the truths of His Word deep within your grandchildren's hearts. Trust that He will use this time together to draw them closer to Himself and strengthen their faith.

These additional keys of success came from what we witnessed during our first few camps. One important key was having help from another family member. For a couple of years, our daughter assisted with two of our earliest Grandkids Camps, and her help was invaluable. Another year, we invited our 13-year-old niece to join us, since the grandchildren attending that year ranged in age from 2 to 10. Given that range, we thought it would be helpful for her to focus mainly on the two-year-old, who could be quite a handful.

Since some camps included grandchildren from both an all-boys family and an all-girls family, we needed to adjust some of the freedoms they were used to at home—like running around naked after bath time. We all know the scenario: A child racing to their room with a towel slipping off or forgetting to close the bathroom door. With curious kids of both genders together, it gave us a good opportunity to teach them about privacy and appropriate behavior.

Now that you have the basics, it's time to plan your Grandkids Camp. Once you have a location set, choose a time that works well for you and your children/grandchildren. Arrange the logistics for dropping off and picking up the kids, while considering how you'll manage car seats—whether by leaving them in the cars or swapping them to make sure you have enough available for day trips. Even if you don't plan on driving anywhere, having car seats on hand is a good idea in case of an emergency.

I inform the parents about any specific items I'd like them to pack for their children, making sure they include essentials like bathing suits, towels, sunscreen, hats, and jackets. They're usually the best judges of what and how much to pack. For example, one year I asked them to send an old T-shirt to use as a paint shirt, which also came in handy for messy baking days and other activities, helping to protect the clothes the kids brought to wear.

Now for the fun part, what you want to read most! Each of the following chapters contains plans for one week of Grandkids Camp, complete with themes, Bible verses to memorize, crafts, activities, snack suggestions, and more. I encourage you to use what resonates most with you—there's no need to do everything. If the idea of a multi-day camp feels overwhelming, consider planning a Grandkids Day instead to test activities out with your grandchildren. Pick your favorite ideas and use them to share meaningful lessons with your grandchildren. No matter how much time you spend, you'll be making a valuable investment in their lives, their futures, and their walks with Jesus. They will cherish these moments forever as my children did, and still do.

My Notes

Grateful/Thankfulness

Introduction

When we held our first Grandkids Camp in 2018, I chose "Grateful" as the theme because I noticed some complaining and a lack of gratitude in my grand-godson and even our two-year-old grandson in recent months. Our first year, we had just 2 children—ages 7 and 2—participating, and I made sure to provide them with a clear definition of the theme word. Grateful means feeling or showing thanks for someone's helpful or kind actions.

Memory Verse: 1 Thessalonians 5:18

"Give thanks in all circumstances, for this is the will of God in Christ Jesus for you."

In addition to that verse, I also incorporated a song based on Psalm 100:4, which goes like this:

I will enter His gates with thanksgiving in my heart; I will enter His courts with praise. I will say, "This is the day that the Lord has made; I will rejoice and be glad in it. He has made me glad; He has made me glad; I will rejoice for He has made me glad." (repeat)

I kept things very simple that week, especially because our two-year-old took an afternoon nap every day, which left only a short window for activities. That quiet time gave our seven-year-old more space to enjoy swimming, fishing, and other outdoor fun with one of us while the little one rested with the other grandparent.

Grateful/Thankfulness: Day One

On the first day, instead of beginning with a full Bible story, you can use the memory verse as a discussion-starter, especially for younger children. Start by introducing the week's theme, along with a clear definition of the theme, then review the memory verse several times with the children to reinforce it. Follow that with a few simple reflection questions to help the children engage with the verse.

Bible Story: Genesis 1-3—Adam and Eve's Sin in the Garden of Eden

Read 1 Thessalonians 5:16–18 aloud and have the children recite it together several times.

Ask: "Have you heard the story of Adam and Eve?"

Explain that Adam and Eve were the first man and woman created by God. In the Garden of Eden, everything was perfect. God provided them with every plant and tree for food—they had everything they needed.

Read Genesis 1:29

Say together: "God gave them everything they needed."

Ask: "Do you think they were thankful for this?"

Next, read Genesis 2:15–17.

Ask: "What did God tell them not to do?"

Follow-Up Question: "If they disobeyed God, what would that be called?" (Answer: sin.)

Ask: “Do you think they remained thankful for everything they had, even though there was one tree they couldn’t eat from?”

Read or summarize Genesis 3:1–10.

Ask: “Did Adam and Eve remain thankful and avoid sin?” (Answer: no.)

Explain: Instead of being thankful for all that God had given them, they focused on what they didn’t have, and they desired the forbidden fruit. Their sin and ours is actually a lack of thankfulness; this was a problem for Adam and Eve because it caused them to be separated from God. Their disobedience introduced sin into the world, separating humanity from God.

What Can Be Done?

This problem cannot be fixed by human effort alone, but God took action. What did He do? He sent His Son, Jesus, to earth to take the punishment that people deserve for their sin and ungrateful hearts. When someone trusts in Jesus, He transforms their heart—replacing an ungrateful heart of stone with a thankful heart of flesh.

Discussion Questions:

1. Are there times when you can’t have certain things that you want? For example, during Grandkids Camp, you might want more playtime, extra dessert, additional screen time, or some new prizes. What might you want but not be able to have?
2. What happens if you don’t get what you want? Are there still things you can be grateful for, even when your desires aren't fulfilled?
3. How is a thankful heart developed?

The greatest gift ever given was God sending His Son, Jesus. Without Jesus in a person’s heart, it is very difficult to truly be thankful. Thankfulness is not just a good habit—it comes from a changed heart in response to the gospel (the good news of what Jesus has done for humanity).

Pause after each question to allow time for thoughtful answers from your grandchildren. This method helps set a meaningful tone for the week, gently addresses a complaining attitude, and points children toward their need for a Savior.

Craft: Paper Plate Donuts

Supplies:

- White paper plates – (with holes cut in the center to resemble donuts — 1 to 2 per child)
- Scissors
- Craft paint
- Paintbrushes (one per child or per color)
- Markers
- Crayons
- Stapler (optional)
- Glue
- White Rice
- Food coloring
- Vinegar
- Real donuts (one per child, from a favorite local donut shop)

Preparation Steps:

1. **Coloring the Rice:**
   Prepare the rice in advance for use as "sprinkles." Three colors are usually enough, and the process is simple:
   a. Measure 1 cup of rice into a container with a lid.
   b. Add 1 teaspoon of vinegar.
   c. Add food coloring—adjust the amount for desired color intensity.

d. Seal the container and shake for 1–2 minutes until the rice is evenly coated.

e. Spread the colored rice on a paper towel or tray to dry (typically takes under an hour).
Once dry, return the rice to containers for later use.

2. **Setting Up the Craft Area:**
Before beginning the activity, cover the work surface with disposable tablecloths—affordable and easily tossed afterward. Just roll up the mess in the tablecloth. Children should wear old T-shirts or smocks to protect their clothing.

3. **Starting the Craft:**
Give each child one or two donut-shaped paper plates. You can ask, "Who likes donuts?"—usually greeted with enthusiastic hands in the air. Children are told that they'll be designing their very own donuts today.

Instructions:

1. Children choose a base color for their donut using paint, markers, or crayons.

2. If using paint, allow time for the plates to dry before adding "sprinkles."
3. For a larger 3D donut, two painted plates can be stapled together around the edges.
4. Once dry, apply glue and sprinkle the colored rice on top as decoration. Expect some mess—leftover rice often becomes a sensory activity. When possible, take the rice outdoors to allow the children to enjoy playing in it like sand.

Reflection and Clean-Up:

While the children work on the donuts, you can gently remind them to focus on what they have—like the donut itself—rather than the hole in the middle, which represents what they might be missing. You might ask, "Are you grateful for donuts?"

After the project, clean up the area and make sure to take photos of the finished paper plate donuts to celebrate their creativity.

Snack: Donuts (of course!)

At snack time, ask once again, "Are you grateful for donuts?" followed by, "Who would like to eat a real donut?"

After the excited responses, the purchased donuts are brought out and handed to each child. This simple moment offers a chance to enjoy a sweet treat while reinforcing the theme of joy and gratitude. The children are encouraged to embrace thankfulness as they enjoy their donuts together.

For children who don't like donuts—or whose parents prefer they skip them—offer "apple donuts" instead. Simply core an apple, slice it into rings, and top with nut butter, raisins, or other fun toppings to give it a donut-like look.

Grateful/Thankfulness: Day Two

Bible Story: Luke 17:11–19 (*The Message Bible*)—The Ten Lepers

At that time in the Bible, leprosy was a serious disease that caused painful skin sores and was highly contagious. Those suffering from leprosy were not only in physical pain but also had to live away from their families and communities to prevent the disease from spreading. They were isolated, lonely, and often forgotten.

In this passage, ten men with leprosy were separated from their loved ones and lived outside the city when they encountered Jesus. When they called out to Him for mercy, He healed all ten of them. As they were returning to their families and villages, only one man returned to thank Jesus for what He had done for him.

Discussion Questions:

1. When do you typically say thank you—to your mom, dad, teacher, friends, or to God?
2. How many lepers were in the story?
3. Where did the lepers go after they were healed?
4. How many were healed?
5. How many returned to thank Jesus?
6. What does that show about gratitude?
7. What was the last thing Jesus said to the man who came back? (Luke17:19)
   "And He said to him, 'Rise and go your way; your faith has made you well.'" Jesus commended him not only for his thankful heart, but also for his faith. Jesus healed him of more than his leprosy.
8. What else did Jesus heal? Jesus changed his heart. God opened the leper's eyes when he was healed to see who Jesus really was.
9. Why did the former leper praise Jesus? Because he realized he was a sinner standing in the presence of the Savior of the world.

Jesus did not praise the man simply for being thankful; He commended him for his **faith**. The man received more than physical healing—Jesus healed his heart. When God opened the man's eyes to who Jesus truly was, his response was to fall at Jesus's feet in worship and gratitude.

Craft: Thank-You Card

Supplies:

- Construction paper

- Crayons
- Markers
- Stickers
- Miscellaneous craft embellishments

In this activity, children create a thank-you card for someone of their choosing. They are encouraged to think about who they want to thank and what they are grateful for. Some may choose to thank a parent, grandparent, teacher, friend—or even make a card for Jesus, if they feel led to do so.

For example, our grandchildren chose to make cards for one or both of their parents, expressing appreciation in their own unique ways.

Once finished, the children can either take their cards home or be given the option to have them mailed.

This simple craft helps reinforce the importance of expressing gratitude in meaningful, personal ways.

Activity: Make Your Own Bubbles and Have a Bubble Party

Children will enjoy making their own giant bubble wands and having a bubble party—a playful, hands-on activity that also connects back to the day's theme of gratitude.

Before beginning, you can explain that bubbles are fun and beautiful, but they don't last long, much like the moments of fun are brief. This reminds children to be thankful for the joy in each moment and to appreciate the good things in their day, even when they don't last forever. And just like we can always make more bubbles, there's always more joy and fun ahead.

Supplies (available at most craft stores):

- 2 wooden dowels per child (or per bubble wand)
- 2 small screw eyes (for tying the string)
- 1 large metal washer

- Cotton string
- Scissors
- Bubble solution
- Bowl or pan for dipping

Instructions:

1. Screw one eye hook into the top of each dowel, making sure it is tightly secured.
2. Cut two lengths of cotton string—one approximately the length of the child's arm and the other the length of both arms stretched out wide.
3. Tie one end of each string to the eye hooks on the dowels. Before tying off the longer string, thread the metal washer through the middle; this helps weigh the string and form larger bubbles.
4. Fill a bowl or tray with bubble solution.
5. Children can take turns dipping their wands into the solution and gently lifting them to create large bubbles. To prevent tangling, allow one child at a time to dip and wave their wand.

Prepare bubble solution using recipe below, though store-bought bubbles can be used as an alternative for convenience. Making the solution at home is simple and cost-effective. The mixture is prepared in a large bowl with a lid to allow for easy storage and future use. However, the excitement of the children led to the solution being used—and spilled—fairly quickly, as they eagerly dove into the fun of bubble play.

To see a video tutorial, check out Inner Child fun - https://innerchildfun.com/2015/05/how-to-make-giant-bubble-wands.html

Recipe for Homemade Bubbles:

- 6 cups distilled water
- 1-2 cup Joy dish soap
- 1-2 tablespoons glycerin

Grateful/Thankfulness: Day Three

Bible Story: Psalm 136—God's Love Endures Forever

Psalm 136 is a powerful chapter that centers on gratitude, repeatedly affirming that *God's love endures forever*. As the children listen to the psalm being read, they are encouraged to list all the things the psalmist gives thanks for—each one a reminder of God's faithful, enduring love.

- God is Good—God's goodness is seen in His constant love, even when people fall short. Romans 5:8 captures this beautifully: *"But God shows His love for us in that while we were still sinners, Christ died for us."* This act of sacrificial love is the ultimate expression of God's goodness.
- God's love endures forever—From the moment of creation; God has shown His love. Even when sin entered the world and broke humanity's relationship with Him, God's love remained, and He made a plan to restore that relationship through Jesus Christ. As John 3:16 tells us: *"For God so loved the world, that He gave His only Son, that whoever believes in Him should not perish but have eternal life."*
- God the Creator—God created the world and everything in it—the sun, moon, and stars—and declared it all "very good" (Genesis 1:31). Though sin disrupted this perfect world, God's love and plan for redemption never changed.
- God the Deliverer—God's enduring love was also demonstrated when He rescued the Israelites from slavery in Egypt, parting the Red Sea and leading them to freedom. In the same way, He sent

Jesus to rescue humanity from slavery to sin, so that people could be restored to relationship with Him.

- God the Powerful—By dividing the Red Sea and leading His people to safety, God showed His mighty power and faithfulness. He remains worthy of worship, trust, and gratitude.

This passage can help your grandchildren see the connection between thankfulness and God's never-ending love. Each act of God described in Psalm 136 is both a reason to be grateful and a reminder of who He is.

Discussion Questions:

1. What kind of things are you thankful for? Help them consider the people, experiences, and blessings in their lives. Encourage them to think deeply—are they thankful for the sacrifice Jesus made on the cross?
2. What reminds you to be thankful? Invite them to identify moments, situations, or even people that prompt them to express gratitude.
3. What things do you forget to be thankful for sometimes? Encourage reflection on the small or everyday blessings that are often taken for granted. Offer examples.
4. How do you say thanks to Mom, Dad, grandparents, or a teacher? This helps them think about the ways they show appreciation to those who love and care for them.
5. How do you say thank you to God? Prompt them to consider how they personally express their gratitude to God—whether through prayer, singing, worship, or showing kindness to others.

Conclude by reminding the children: *The best way to say thank you to God is by following Him and choosing to obey Him.*

Activity: Nature Walk of Gratitude

Head out for a peaceful walk in nature and take time to notice everything worth appreciating—the breeze, the birds, the sunlight through the trees.

As you walk, collect some things you're most grateful for. Choose a few favorites to reflect on later. Along the way, keep an eye out for a smooth, well-shaped rock—perfect for painting as the activity here will show.

Our Experience:

I gave each child a bag and asked them to collect things they felt thankful for, with a special emphasis on finding a good rock to paint. Our grand-godson kept spotting large rocks that were still partially buried and insisted on trying to dig them up. After some effort, he finally found one that was just the right size—easy to carry and above ground.

At one point, he excitedly unearthed what he believed was a treasure and announced he was going to wear it as a hat. Just before he put it on his head, I took a closer look and realized it was actually an old dog dish, and I quickly stopped him. We still took the dog dish home, where he cleaned it, painted it proudly, and took it with him—completely delighted, even though he didn't have a dog. He found gratitude in the little things, even a discarded item in the woods.

Craft: Thankfulness Rock Painting

For this activity, children will paint a rock with something they're thankful for as a way to reflect on gratitude.

Supplies:

- A rock collected during the nature walk
- Paintbrushes
- Paint (any color)
- Drop cloth or an outdoor painting area
- Water for rinsing brushes

Grateful/Thankfulness: Day Four

Bible Story: Exodus 15:1–19—The Song of the Sea

Context Leading Up to Exodus 15:1–19:

Before the Israelites sang the Song of the Sea, they had just experienced one of the most dramatic moments in their journey from Egypt. After escaping slavery, they found themselves in a desperate situation—trapped between the Red Sea ahead of them and the Egyptian army closing in from behind. Their escape seemed impossible.

In this moment of fear and uncertainty, God performed a remarkable miracle. He parted the Red Sea, allowing the Israelites to walk safely through on dry ground. Once they had crossed, the Egyptian army pursued them into the sea. Then, at God's command, the waters returned to their normal state, drowning the Egyptians and securing the Israelites' deliverance.

Exodus 15:1–19 captures the Israelites' immediate response to this miracle. Led by Moses, they sang a song of praise and gratitude to God. This song celebrated God's power, faithfulness, and protection, recognizing Him as their deliverer.

Read Exodus 15:1–19

Discussion Questions:

1. How did the Israelites praise and thank God in Exodus 15:1-19? What specific actions or words did they use to honor God?
2. How would you feel if you were saved in such a powerful way? Would you respond with gratitude and praise?
3. Did you know this story also points to how God saves us today? Just as God delivered the Israelites from slavery in Egypt, He offers to deliver each of us from the slavery of sin. God sent Jesus to set us free, and because of this, we too can sing songs of joy and gratitude.

You can expand on the gospel presentation as appropriate for the age of the children.

Craft: Homemade musical instrument to use in praising God

Supplies:

- Plastic spoon
- Plastic Easter eggs
- Empty toilet paper or paper towel rolls
- Wax paper
- Rubber bands
- Popping corn
- Dried beans
- Fun tape (I found tape at the craft store that said "grateful" on it.)

Spoon and Egg Maracas:

Instructions:

1. Fill plastic Easter eggs with popping corn or dried beans. Each type will produce a slightly different sound.
2. Take two plastic spoons and place them on either side of the egg, facing it.
3. Secure the spoons to the egg with fun tape, using the tape to wrap around the spoons and the egg, forming a handle.
4. Let the kids use different colors of tape or other decorations to personalize their maracas.

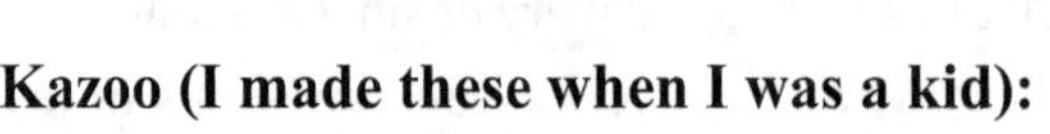

Kazoo (I made these when I was a kid):

Instructions:

1. Take an empty toilet paper roll or paper towel roll.
2. Allow the children to decorate the roll if you have time.
3. Cut a small piece of wax paper and cover one end of the roll. Fold the edges of the wax paper slightly over the outside of the roll.
4. Secure the wax paper with a rubber band around the roll.
5. Have the children hum into the open end of the roll (without wax paper). Emphasize making musical sounds rather than yelling or screaming.

Worship Activity: Singing with Instruments

After making their instruments, the children can use them to sing songs and worship God—mirroring the way the Israelites praised God in Exodus 15; you can lead them in a simple worship song based on Exodus 15:1–2. This connection helps the children engage with the biblical story in a meaningful and joyful way. Any age-appropriate worship song can be used for this activity. The goal is to encourage children to express gratitude and praise through music, reinforcing the theme of worship and deliverance found in the story.

Reflections:

Throughout the week, I tried to consistently apply the truths we were learning. Whenever the grandchildren started to complain about something, I gently reminded them to be thankful and redirected their focus. One way I helped them remember was by asking, "What is our verse this week?"—a simple prompt that encouraged them to review and reinforce the verse in their hearts. I'd also ask, "Do you want to pray and ask God to give you a grateful heart?" or "Are you being grateful right now? How can you start to be grateful?"

It wasn't always easy, and I know how hard it can be for children (and adults) to feel thankful when things aren't going their way. But those moments became teachable ones, revealing how much we need God to change our hearts and help us become truly grateful.

One example stands out from my experience: It was an extremely hot day during Grandkids Camp, and I was tempted to complain myself. Instead, we encouraged the kids to focus on what they could be thankful for, asking questions like, "Can you be grateful that you're able to be outside?" or "Can you appreciate that God gave your hands to make this craft or feet to explore the woods?" These simple prompts helped the children (and me!) stay grounded in the theme of gratitude

Love

Introduction

Having successfully completed our first year of Grandkids Camp, I was ready to plan year two. At that point, I decided to make the theme of the camp, "the Fruit of the Spirit," focusing on one specific fruit each year moving forward; the remainder of this book is written to follow that plan. That way, we could revisit each theme and many of the activities once we had gone through all the fruits.

My plan was for the older children to help guide the younger ones with their projects before starting on their own.

Memory Verse: John 13:34

"*A new commandment I give to you, that you love one another: just as I have loved you, you also are to love one another.*"

Songs – "Jesus Loves Me" and "Jesus Loves the Little Children"

Love: Day One

Bible Lesson: What is Love?

Today's lesson is to introduce the topic of love. In order to do that, ask the children the following questions and talk about what love really is. The depth of information that can be shared about love will need to be tailored to the ages of the children.

Discussion Questions:

1. What does the Bible say about love?
   God is love, and love originates from Him. He loves everyone and has a wonderful plan for each life (1 John 4:7-11; John 10:10).
2. Does God love us even when we do wrong or feel grumpy?
   God's love is unconditional. He demonstrated the greatest act of love by sending Jesus while humanity was still separated from Him by sin (Romans 5:8).
3. What did Jesus do to demonstrate His love?
   Jesus died on the cross, taking the punishment for all the wrongs and sins people have committed (1 Peter 2:24; 2 Corinthians 5:21).
4. How can we love God?
   By accepting what Jesus did for us and acknowledging that we are sinners separated from God without Him (John 1:12).
5. How can we love others?
   By embracing God's love for us and living for Him, we can see others through God's eyes and share His love with them (John 13:34-35).
6. Do you love your family and siblings?
7. Encourage the children to reflect on the love they have for their families.
8. Are there people who are hard to love?
   Loving certain people can be challenging, but God loves everyone and calls us to do the same (Luke 6:32-36).
9. Who should we love?

We are called to love God, ourselves, family, friends, neighbors, and even those who are difficult to love (Matthew 22:36-40).

10. What about enemies?
    While it is hoped there are none, remind them that sometimes we may not get along with others. Ask God to help them love those who mistreat them or hold different beliefs, trusting that God will guide them to show love as He has shown His love for us (Luke 6:32-36).

Activity: Mini Golf

Find a fun activity nearby to participate and watch for opportunities to show love to those around. We chose mini golf. I recommend avoiding a visit when it's 90 degrees outside—it really dampened the fun. Honestly, there wasn't much "love" for mini golf during that sweltering outing, but the children did well in not complaining and showing love to one another.

Thankfully, the ice cream shop next door offered a sweet escape!

Snack: Ice Cream

Who Loves Ice Cream?

What child doesn't adore ice cream? Take the children to their favorite local ice cream shop where they can pick their flavor. Consider bringing the fun home by buying ice cream and toppings to create personalized sundaes. Sharing a favorite flavor with someone else becomes a simple yet meaningful way to show love and make the treat even more special.

Love: Day Two

Bible Story: Luke 10:25-37—The Parable of the Good Samaritan

Before sharing the story, explain to the children that Jesus teaches us to "love our neighbor as ourselves." When someone asked, "Who is our neighbor?" Jesus responded with the parable of the Good Samaritan. This story beautifully illustrates what it means to demonstrate the kind of love God desires for everyone to show.

Read Luke 10:25-37

Discussion Questions:

1. What did the first man, a church leader, do? Did he show love?
2. What action did the Levite take? Did he show love?
3. At the end, Jesus asked, "Who do you think was the good neighbor?" Who do you think had God's love to show compassion to the man in the road?
4. Jesus told us to go and show love like the Samaritan. Do you do this?
5. Love and compassion see the needs of other people, and their greatest need is the gospel —to know about Jesus. Who have you noticed that is in need?
6. How have you shown love by helping someone?
7. Have you received God's love and compassion so you can show it to others?

The only way we can truly show love and compassion is by receiving the love and compassion that God has offered to us through His son, Jesus.

Craft: Ice Packs

Sometimes when someone gets hurt, using an ice pack can really help. In this activity, children will create their own ice packs, which they may be able to use later if someone they know gets injured.

Supplies:

- Snack-size resealable plastic bags (1 per child)
- Various colors of felt or fabric
- Scissors
- Glue sticks

- Small sponges (1 per child) that fit inside the plastic bag
- Bowl or cup of water

Instructions:

1. **Prepare the Bags:** Provide each child with a resealable bag and a piece of felt or fabric.
2. **Cut the Felt:** Instruct the children to cut the felt into squares large enough to cover the bag. They may use one large square or several smaller ones.
3. **Glue the Felt:** Assist the kids in gluing the felt onto one or both sides of the bag.
4. **Wet the Sponges:** After the felt is attached, give each child a sponge and have them dip it into the water until fully saturated.
5. **Squeeze and Seal:** Help the children squeeze out most of the water from the sponges and place them inside their bags. Seal the bags securely.
6. **Freeze or chill the bag:** This will act like an ice pack that can be used on bumps or bruises.
7. **Clean Up:** Keep a towel nearby to handle any spills or drips during the activity.

Explain that they can choose when to use them. If someone gets a bump and begins to cry, one of the children may offer their homemade ice pack to help provide comfort.

Activity: Acting Out the Story of the Good Samaritan

This activity provides an engaging way for children to act out the story of the Good Samaritan, while incorporating the ice pack made earlier.

Characters:

- Narrator
- Traveler (hurt man)
- Robbers
- Priest

- Levite
- Good Samaritan

Props:

- Ice pack (from previous activity)
- Blanket or mat
- Simple costumes or props, such as hats, scarves, or robes

Setup:

The narrator begins by introducing the story, explaining that a traveler was going down a road when he was attacked by robbers.

The traveler walks down the road minding his own business.

The robbers sneak up on the traveler, pretend to attack him, and then quickly run away. They leave him lying on the road.

The priest walks by, notices the injured traveler, and shakes his head before crossing to the other side of the path without offering help.

The Levite follows, also observing the injured man, but chooses to pass by without stopping.

The Good Samaritan enters, notices the traveler, and expresses concern.

Action:

The Good Samaritan kneels beside the traveler and checks on him. He takes out the ice pack and says, "I have something to help you feel better!" He gently places the ice pack on the traveler's injury.

Then the Good Samaritan helps the traveler sit up and offers kind and comforting words.

Conclusion:

The narrator concludes the activity by reminding the group that the Good Samaritan showed love and kindness when others did not. Participants are encouraged to reflect on ways they can show love and help others in their own lives.

Adaptations to the dialogue or actions may be made to suit the needs or age of the group.

Craft: Wine Bottle Vase

Children can create a wine bottle vase to give as a gift to someone they want to show love to or to serve as a personal reminder to love others, reflecting the love God has shown. Heart shapes or the word "LOVE" can be incorporated into the design using painter's tape, but each child is encouraged to express their creativity in their own way.

Supplies:

- One empty wine bottle (with labels removed) per child
- Blue painter's tape (easy to remove)
- Various colors of spray paint (children may select their preferred colors)
- Fresh, dried, or artificial flowers (optional)

Instructions:

1. **Preparation**: All wine bottles should be clean and free of labels before beginning the project.
2. **Design**: Children apply painter's tape to the bottles to create unique designs. They are encouraged to be creative while focusing on the theme of love. Some may choose to tape a heart shape or spell out the word "LOVE" as part of their design.
3. **Spray Painting**: The group moves outdoors to apply the first coat of spray paint to the bottles. Once painted, the bottles should be left to dry for a few hours.

4. **Second Coat**: After the initial coat has dried, a second layer of spray paint can be applied. The bottles should then be left to dry completely, preferably overnight.
5. **Remove Tape**: Once fully dry, the tape is carefully removed to reveal the final designs.
6. **Finishing Touch**: Completed vases may be sent home with artificial flowers as a finishing detail, if desired.

Love: Day Three

Bible Story: Luke 19:1-10—The Story of Zacchaeus

Before sharing the story, ask the children who they would be thrilled to have spend the night at their house and why they chose that friend or fictional character. Discuss ways to make guests feel welcome in their homes.

Read Luke 19:1-10 or from *The Jesus Storybook Bible* the story titled "The Man Who Didn't Have Any Friends (None)."

Discussion Questions:

Although Zacchaeus was known as a sinful tax collector, he desired to see Jesus when He came to town. This raises the question of whether people who seem unkind, mean, or difficult still desire friendship and love, even if they don't always show it. The story illustrates how Jesus reaches out to those who feel unloved, and His love transforms Zacchaeus's heart and has the power to transform anyone's heart.

1. Have you ever climbed a tree? Was it easy? How high do you think Zacchaeus had to climb to see Jesus over the crowd?
2. Can you think of anyone who might be hard to love? How can you start showing them kindness?
3. How would you feel if you didn't have any friends?

4. Do you think the actions of the people in the story demonstrated love?
5. Should people who make mistakes still receive love?
6. Have you ever made a mistake (sinned)?
7. Despite Zacchaeus's wrongdoings, did Jesus still treat him with kindness? Why do you think that is? Remember, He loves Zacchaeus just as He loves you, even when you make mistakes.
8. How did God show His love for us even though we made and still make mistakes? He sent His son Jesus to take the punishment we deserve. Jesus is our perfect example of how to love and show kindness, even to those who do bad things.

Craft: Paper Bag Trees

Supplies:

- Brown paper lunch bags
- Green construction paper for leaves
- Glue
- Scissors

Instructions:

1. Begin by cutting slits into the brown paper bag at the opening end, then stand each bag upright.
2. The bottom of the bag is twisted to form the tree's base. If needed, some paper can be stuffed into the bottom for added stability.
3. Sections of the bag are then twisted together at the slits to create branches.
4. Next, green construction paper is torn or cut into small pieces to serve as leaves. A dot of glue is applied to the tip of each leaf before attaching it to the tree, holding it for a few seconds until secure.
5. For added creativity, a figure of Zacchaeus can be drawn and cut out to place in the tree.

Craft: Jesus Knows and Loves Me Sign

Supplies:

- Printed card stock with "Jesus Knows and Loves Me" at the top (one per child)
- Thin painter's tape
- Various colors of paint
- Sponges or shapes for painting

Instructions:

1. Children begin by using thin painter's tape to spell out their names on the printed card stock.
2. Next, sponges or shapes are dipped into paint and used to cover the taped letters, taking care not to paint over the printed words at the top. For very young children who might accidentally paint over the phrase, additional tape can be applied to protect "Jesus Knows and Loves Me."
3. Once the paint is completely dry, the tape is carefully removed to reveal the children's names underneath.

This activity demonstrates that even when others may not know or see them, Jesus always knows their name and loves them.

Activity: Find Your Animal Friend Game

Supplies:

- Paper
- Markers

Instructions:

1. Animal names are written on pieces of paper, focusing on animals whose sounds children can easily mimic, such as dog, cat, cow, and others. Two pieces of paper are created for each animal name.

For non-readers, pictures of the animals can also be included on the paper.

2. Children are informed that there is someone else in the room with the same animal's name, and they need to find their partner by making the sound of their animal. For example, a cow would moo, and a cat would meow, but no other words are allowed.
3. Once partners find each other, they hook arms to show they have paired up.
4. Grandparents are encouraged to join in the fun as well. If the children enjoy the game, multiple rounds can be played by collecting the slips of paper and redistributing them.

Even in a noisy crowd, Zacchaeus was seen, and Jesus called him by name. Just like you found your animal partner by calling out and listening for their sound, Jesus sees you, knows you, and hears you when you call out to Him.

Activity: Play "Pin Zacchaeus on the Tree" similar to "Pin the Tail on the Donkey"

Supplies:

- Large piece of paper to draw a large tree
- Plain white paper for Zacchaeus
- Green paper for leaves
- Paint (for the tree) or markers
- Painter's tape (for easy removal)

Instructions:

1. **Create the Tree:** In advance, paint a tree with plenty of branches on a large piece paper or posterboard. Be sure to include branches where Zacchaeus can "sit." Tape the tree to the wall at the children's eye level.

2. **Prepare Zacchaeus:** Draw Zacchaeus in a sitting position. Card stock works well for a sturdier Zacchaeus.
3. **Add Leaves:** Before starting the game, invite the children to decorate the tree by adding leaves. They can use cut-out shapes or draw directly on the tree.
4. **Play the Game:** Use painter's tape to attach Zacchaeus to the tree. Each child will take turns trying to "pin" Zacchaeus on a branch (using tape). For an added challenge, blindfold older children as you would in "Pin the Tail on the Donkey."
5. **Game Duration:** Allow each child to have multiple turns, keeping the game going as long as they enjoy it. This activity can also serve as a fun distraction while you prepare meals or clean up.

Song: Zacchaeus Was a Wee Little Man

Author: unknown

Zacchaeus was a wee little man. A wee little man was he
(Pat gently like patting on a child's head)
He climbed up in the sycamore tree, For the Lord he wanted to see.
(Make climbing motions)
And as the Savior came along, He looked up in the tree,
(Shield your eyes and look up)
And He said, "Zacchaeus, you come down;"
(Point your finger and shake it as you say this)
For I'm going to your house today, for I'm going to your house today (or we said "for tea").

And Zacchaeus came down from that tree, and he said,
"What a better man I'll be. I'll give my money to the poor."
What a better man I'll be. What a better man I'll be.

(Repeat motions where appropriate)

The last verse I found online, but I don't remember singing it as a child. We always did motions to the song, so they are in italics.

Activity: Climb a Tree

Go climb a tree so the children can see how difficult it might have been. If the children are still quite young, they could scale a playset and imagine it as a tree, pretending they're waiting for Jesus to appear.

Craft: Love Ribbon Heart

Supplies:

- Pink or red paper (cut into heart shapes) or paper plates (to color and cut into a heart)
- Colored ribbons that can be written on (6-8 inches long each)
- Stapler or tape
- Crayons or markers
- String for hanging

Instructions:

1. Give each child 5-7 ribbons. On each ribbon, they should write the names of people they love. Encourage them to include names of those who might be harder to love as a reminder. It will be easy for them to add Mom, Dad, siblings, etc.
2. After decorating their hearts, attach the ribbons to the bottom using a stapler or tape.
3. Poke a hole at the top of the heart and thread the string through for hanging.
4. Consider adding the phrase "Love one another" on the heart for inspiration.

Activity: Heart-Shaped Sugar Cookies

Make the cookies and bake them prior to dinner so they will be cooled and ready to decorate right after dinner. This makes for an enticing dessert and fun project after dinner.

Supplies:

- Sugar cookie dough (I used store-bought for convenience)
- Rolling pin
- Flour
- Mat for rolling out dough
- Heart-shaped cookie cutters
- Baking sheets
- Premade frosting (I used store-bought)
- Sprinkles and other decorations

Instructions:

1. Roll out the sugar cookie dough on a floured mat using a rolling pin.
2. Use heart-shaped cookie cutters to cut out the cookies and place them on baking sheets.
3. Bake according to the dough instructions and let them cool completely.
4. After dinner, give each child their own cookie, along with a bowl of frosting to spread on top.
5. Allow them to decorate with sprinkles and other toppings as they like.
6. Capture photos of their creations before they enjoy their delicious treats!
7. There will be plenty of cookies left for the next day's enjoyment.

This fun activity not only makes for a delightful dessert but also creates lasting memories for everyone!

Love: Day Four

Bible Lesson: John 3:16 and Romans 5:5

Object Lessons: God's Big Love[1]

Supplies:

- Adult shoes
- Child's shoes (a baby shoe works even better)
- Seed packet
- Plant or small tree
- Ping pong ball
- Beach ball

Instructions:

Gather all the items in a large bag beforehand to keep the children from getting distracted by the items.

The goal of this activity is to help the children understand that God's love is beyond our imagination. While He can reside in a child's heart, His love is vast enough to embrace the entire world. Grasping this concept can be difficult for anyone, especially a child. Convey the truth about God's ability to love "big" with these three, easy-to-use object lessons. Visual aids make demonstrating these special attributes easier than ever, as each lesson can be connected to love and the verses from this day (John 3:15 and Romans 5:5).

Daddy Shoes and Baby Shoes: Show God's bigness by presenting the baby shoes while keeping the adult shoes hidden. Discuss how small the baby shoes are and relate them to our hearts. You might say, "When we

---

[1]Adapted From "God's Big Love Object Lesson," by Mimi Patrick, Ministry-to-Children by Tony Kumer, (https://ministry-to-children.com/gods-big-love-object-lessons/) - Copyright © 2025 **Creative Commons Attribution-ShareAlike 4.0 International**.

love someone, we often think that love is really big. But compared to God's love, our love is very small." Next, reveal the adult shoes and explain, "These shoes represent God's big love." Place the adult shoes next to the baby shoes, then say, "Look how small our love appears next to God's! His love is so vast that He can love everyone at the same time. Can you do that?" In order to love others at all, we need to have God's love change our hearts.

Seeds and trees: For this object lesson, you'll need a packet of small seeds and a potted tree or large plant (a live tree is ideal, as kids are very observant). Start by discussing how tall the tree will grow. Invite each child to stand next to the tree, one at a time, comparing their heights to the tree. Then, sprinkle some seeds into the children's hands and explain that these tiny seeds represent God's love.

When we accept Jesus, God's love is like planting a seed in our hearts. Just as the seeds can grow into large trees, God's love grows within us. Before we invite Him into our hearts, our love is small like these seeds. After we invite Him into our hearts, we can love big, just like God does.

Ping pong ball and a giant beach ball: Use this fun activity to illustrate the difference between human love and God's love in a playful way. Start by showing the ping pong ball while keeping the beach ball hidden, as revealing it too early might distract the kids from the lesson. Bounce the ping pong ball on the table and say, "I love all of you so much! So do your friends. But as great as our love is, God's love is so much bigger. Let's see what that looks like!"

Then, reveal the beach ball and bounce it up and down, explaining, "God's love is like this huge beach ball—it's immense and reaches everywhere!" Spend some time bouncing the ball back and forth with the kids, allowing them to enjoy the fun. Wrap up by letting everyone have fun playing with the beach ball.

Craft: Plant seeds

This activity is to help watch their plants grow and remember how big God's love is for them.

A self-watering seed starter pot can be made by repurposing 2-liter bottles.

Supplies:

- 2-liter plastic bottles (one for each child or family, if you prefer)
- Potting soil
- Seeds (I used beans, but flowers or herbs work well too.)
- Scissors or a knife
- Vegetable oil and paper towels

Instructions:

1. **Clean the Bottle:** Remove any labels and leftover glue from the bottle before you take out the scissors. Household items including vegetable oil, margarine, and peanut butter can be used with a paper towel to remove the sticky residue left over from the label. I have also used lemon essential oil or Goo Gone®.
2. **Cut the Bottle in Half:** Using scissors or a knife, cut the bottle in half about 5 inches from the bottom. An adult should do this part and be careful of the sharp edges of the bottle.
3. **Make Water Holes:** Take the 2-liter bottle and puncture eight holes around the top, about 1-inch apart from each other. It's important to puncture enough holes so that your plant can get the right amount of water needed to help it grow. You can use a metal skewer to poke holes or use a knife.
4. **Add Potting Soil and Water:** Flip the top half of the bottle over and fill it with about 3 cups of damp potting soil. Make sure not to overfill it so there is enough room to plant your seeds at the end. Afterward, fill the bottom half of the bottle with water and place the top half of the bottle, neck down, into the water.

5. **Finishing Touches:** Plant some seeds in the potting soil and lightly water. Place outside if it is warm enough or inside where it can get proper sunlight. Beans germinate quickly; that is why I select this type of seed. They can also grow pretty tall.

Reflections

Reinforcing the message to "love one another" is essential during your time together. While we didn't encounter any issues with the three children this year, I anticipate that typical disagreements may arise as they grow older. Consistently reminding them to "love one another" can help diffuse arguments and conflicts while pointing them to God's love for them.

This theme is perfect for sharing the gospel and highlighting God's greatest gift of love—salvation—at any time throughout the week as you encourage them to "love one another," just as Jesus has loved them.

Joy

Introduction

This third year of Grandkids Camp theme was "Building Joy," and we embraced a construction zone motif to convey that message. I'm always on the lookout for coloring sheets, crafts, or other supplies that can help reinforce our theme.

Memory Verse: Psalm 47:1

"*Clap your hands, all peoples! Shout to God with loud songs of joy*!"

Songs

"Joy, Joy, Joy, Joy down in my heart."[2]

This is such a fun song.

I've got the joy, joy, joy, joy down in my heart.

(shout) Where?

---

[2] "Joy, Joy, Joy, Joy down in my heart," by George William Cooke, 1925

Down in my heart.

(shout) Where?

Down in my heart.

I've got the joy, joy, joy, joy down in my heart.

Down in my heart to stay.

There are other verses, but we just did this one. There was an old worship song from when I was in high school based on Psalm 47:1.

There is a cute YouTube video for kids with this song, which can be found here: https://www.youtube.com/watch?v=Phel2mKdsSo

Joy: Day One

Bible Story: Acts 8:26-40—The Ethiopian Rejoices

Discussion Questions:

1. Has an angel ever spoken to you?
2. What did the angel tell Philip to do? The angel instructed Philip to go south to the road that leads from Jerusalem to Gaza.
3. Would you be like Philip and do what the angel said?
4. What was the Ethiopian reading? He was reading from the book of Isaiah.
5. What did Philip ask the Ethiopian? Philip asked the Ethiopian if he understood what he was reading.
6. Who did God send to help this man understand what Isaiah wrote? God sent Philip to explain the Scriptures to him.
7. What did the Ethiopian ask Philip? He asked about whom the prophet was speaking— himself or someone else.

8. After Philip told the Ethiopian the good news about Jesus, what did the Ethiopian ask? He asked if there was anything to stop him from being baptized.
9. After the Ethiopian was baptized, what did he do? He went on his way rejoicing.
10. Where did Philip go? Philip found himself in Azotus and continued to preach the gospel in all the towns until he reached Caesarea.
11. This story is a great example of how God prepares people to hear the good news about Jesus. Nothing will cause more rejoicing than someone accepting that Jesus has forgiven their sins and that they wish to follow Him. Baptizing is a way to show everyone that you have decided to follow Jesus.

Craft/Activity: Rainbow with Pot of Gold

Supplies:

- Paper
- Scissors
- Rainbow-colored crepe paper
- Glue
- Gold pot (I spray-painted a small bucket.)
- Printed Bible verses on paper, cut apart—at least one verse for each child.
  Examples of verses: Isaiah 41:10, Deuteronomy 31:8, Jeremiah 29:11, Exodus 20:12, James 1:5. These are just a few of the many wonderful promises in God's Word.

Instructions:

1. Create a rainbow on the paper using crepe paper or let younger children color their own rainbows. Share the saying that "at the end of every rainbow is a pot of gold," emphasizing that God's

Word and the Good News of the Gospel is even more valuable than gold.

2. Prepare the pot of gold filled with verses inside.
3. Have each child draw a verse from the "pot of gold" and read it aloud or read it for themselves. Discuss the promise found in each verse.
4. Conclude by reading Psalm 19:9b-11 (ESV): "*The rules of the Lord are true and righteous altogether. More to be desired are they than gold, even much fine gold; sweeter also than honey and drippings of the honeycomb. Moreover, by them is your servant warned; in keeping them there is great reward.*"

Snack: Rainbow Fruit Bites

Supplies:

- Thin stick pretzels (very thin)
- Fruit Loops cereal
- Mini marshmallows

Instructions:

Have the children string colored Fruit Loops onto the thin stick pretzels, then add mini marshmallows on each end to hold everything together. If the pretzels are too thick (as ours were), this may not work as planned, but no worries! They can either stack the Fruit Loops or lay them out to create a rainbow shape, using marshmallows at each end to represent little clouds. Toothpicks or wooden skewers can also be used if preferred. Enjoy!

Snack: Rainbow Treat

Supplies:

- White frosting (tinted blue)
- Graham crackers or similar size sugar cookie
- Airheads (in rainbow colors)

- Mini marshmallows
- Mini Reese's

Instructions:

1. **Frost the Graham Crackers:** Spread a layer of blue frosting evenly over each graham cracker or cookie.
2. **Shape the Airheads:** Take the Airheads and bend them into an arch to create the rainbow shape. They will need to be cut to smaller sizes so they will stand up.

3. **Secure the Rainbow:** Use additional frosting to attach the ends of the Airheads to the frosted graham cracker.
4. **Add Marshmallow Clouds:** For stability, place mini marshmallows at each end of the graham cracker to act as clouds. This will help support the rainbow.
5. **Add a Mini Reese's:** This will represent a pot of gold for a sweet touch of fun.

Joy: Day Two

Bible Story: Luke 15:8-10 and Psalm 32:1-5, 11—Joyful Celebrations

Discussion Questions:

1. Have you ever lost something that was important to you? What actions did you take to find it?
2. How many coins did the woman in the parable possess?
3. Would you care if you lost just one coin out of ten?
4. Why do you think the woman in the story cared about losing one coin?

5. What is said to happen in heaven when a sinner repents? Heaven rejoices when someone repents and chooses to follow Jesus.
6. In Psalm 32, how did David express his feelings when he kept silent about his sin?
7. How do you feel when you know you have sinned?
8. How do you feel once you confess your sins?
9. What does David say at the end after he has confessed his sin? He was joyful, because confessing and following Jesus is the only way to find true, lasting joy.
10. Have you confessed your sins to God and accepted Jesus's sacrifice for your sins?

Craft: Joy Painting

Supplies:

- One canvas for each child (approximately 5x7 or 6x8 inches)
- Various colored acrylic craft paints
- One paintbrush for each child
- Painter's tape or letter stickers for "JOY"

Instructions:

1. **Prepare the Canvas**: Use painter's tape to spell out the word "JOY" on the canvas. Ensure the tape is pressed down firmly to prevent paint from seeping underneath. If you can find sticker letters that fit the canvas, you can spell out JOY in larger letters.
2. **Choose Colors**: Let the children select two different colors of paint for their project.
3. **First Layer**: With the first color, instruct the children to cover the entire canvas, including the letters, using gentle strokes. Encourage them to avoid going back and forth too much to keep the letters in place.
4. **Drying Time**: Allow the first layer of paint to dry completely.

5. **Second Layer**: Once dry, take a dry paintbrush and dip it into a small amount of the second paint color. Brush off excess paint on a paper towel (this step can be done by a grandparent if needed). Then, hand the brush to the children and have them lightly paint over the entire canvas.
6. **Reveal the Letters**: After the second layer is dry, carefully remove the painter's tape or stickers to reveal the word JOY on the canvas.

Reflection:

As we reveal each letter, let us remember that true joy comes from following Jesus and obeying His commands. Just as the letters spelling "JOY" are hidden beneath layers, our genuine joy is concealed by sin. When Jesus removes the layers of sin from our lives, we can experience the fullness of joy. This joy is not merely a fleeting emotion but a deep, abiding peace that comes from being in a right relationship with God. As the apostle Paul writes, *"Rejoice in the Lord always"* (Philippians 4:4), reminding us that our joy is rooted in our connection with Christ.

Until that day, when all is revealed, true joy remains hidden, much like the letters beneath the surface. But as we walk with Jesus and allow Him to cleanse us, we uncover the joy that He has set before us. This joy is not dependent on our circumstances but on our relationship with Him, who is the source of all joy.

Activity: Nature Walk/Treasure Hunt–Finding Joy in Nature

Objective: No complaining allowed on these walks in the woods. Just joy in God's nature.

Instructions:

1. **Preparation:**

   a. Provide each child with a small bag to collect their treasures—this could be a small backpack or a reusable tote.
   b. Remind them that they can collect items such as flowers, rocks, leaves, acorns, and other natural finds.
2. **Set the Rules:**
   a. Explain that the goal of the walk is to find joy in nature.
   b. Establish a rule that no complaining is allowed during the walk. Encourage positive observations and sharing of joyful moments.
3. **Nature Walk:**
   a. Head out on a designated trail or into a nearby wooded area.
   b. Encourage the children to take their time, observe their surroundings, and appreciate the beauty around them.
4. **Collecting Treasures:**
   a. As they walk, let the children gather items that catch their eye.
   b. Encourage them to think about what makes each item special or unique.
5. **Reflection:**
   a. Once the walk is complete, gather the group and allow each child to share what they found.
   b. Discuss what they loved about the experience and how it felt to focus on the joys of nature.

This activity not only fosters a love for the outdoors but also encourages joy and gratitude for the beauty of God's creation.

Snack: Dirt Cups with Worms for a Construction Zone of Joy

Your grandkids will love digging through their "dirt" to find the gummy worms—it's sure to be a delightful and memorable treat! We used to make this for our kids when they were in elementary school, and it was always a big hit!

Here's a simple recipe that brings joy to any occasion.

Supplies:

- Clear plastic cups (1 per child): The clear cups allow you to see the layers
- 2 cups cold milk
- 1 package Oreos (crushed into crumbs)
- 1 package (4 oz) instant chocolate pudding
- 1 (8 oz) package Cool Whip
- Gummy worms

Instructions:

1. **Mix the Pudding:**
    a. Pour the cold milk into a mixing bowl and add the instant pudding mix.
    b. Whisk together until well blended.
    c. Let the pudding sit for about 5 minutes to thicken.
2. **Combine with Cool Whip:**
    a. Gently fold the Cool Whip into the pudding until the mixture is uniform in color.
3. **Crush the Oreos:**
    a. Place Oreos in a large zip bag and crush them. This is a fun task for the kids!

4. **Layer the Cups:**
    a. Start by adding about 1 tablespoon of crushed Oreos to the bottom of each cup.
    b. Next, layer in the chocolate pudding.
    c. Repeat the layers of Oreos and pudding until the cups are filled.
5. **Hide the Worms:**
    a. For a fun surprise, place gummy worms in one of the layers instead of on top, so the kids have to dig to find them.
6. **Finish Off:**
    a. Top with a final layer of crushed Oreos.
    b. Chill in the refrigerator or enjoy immediately if the kids can't wait!

My grandkids liked the worms better than the dirt pudding, though some of them weren't sure about the worms.

Activity: Bubbles

We had such a great time with bubbles the first year that we decided to make it an annual tradition! This year, I bought some new bubble wands, but unfortunately, many of them didn't work as well as the regular wands and the string ones we used previously.

We also incorporated a little lesson about bubbles: They bring us so much joy to see, chase, and pop, but once they're gone, we can still find happiness in the memories. This reflects life as well—while our joyful experiences may not last forever, we can cherish the moments we had and carry that joy with us even after they're gone. We can also know that the joy of the Lord never leaves us like the bubbles popping. When we have Jesus in our hearts, there will always be joy available to us.

The rest of the morning was spent swimming at the state park beach. I bought each of the kids their own bucket and shovel to play with. We packed a lunch to bring along, so when we returned at nap time, they were all set to rest. It's funny how kids who claim they don’t like peanut butter and jelly sandwiches can devour a whole one in no time when that’s the only option available!

Joy: Day Three

Bible Story: Luke 15:11–31—The Parable of the Prodigal Son

Discussion Questions:

1. Why do you think the son wanted to leave home?
2. Where did his journey take him?
3. Was he looking for joy?
4. Did he find joy in his pursuits?
5. How might the father have felt when his son left?
6. If you left home, how do you think your parents would feel?
7. Where did the son finally decide to go?
8. What made him decide to go home?
9. What was the father's response when his son returned, and why?
10. Where are you seeking joy?
11. What do you think will bring you joy?
12. Where do you think joy is best found? In following Jesus.

Just as the father joyfully welcomes his son back home in the parable, Jesus extends grace and welcomes you when you return to Him with a repentant heart. The prodigal son sought joy in worldly pleasures—only to find emptiness and despair. His journey reflects the futility of seeking lasting happiness in fleeting things. But true joy is found not in what the world offers, but in the enduring love and forgiveness Jesus extends to you.

Craft: Homemade Playdough

Since the kids were quite young, I prepared the playdough in advance and stored different colors and textures in zip-lock bags. For our construction zone theme, I even made a batch that resembled dirt. At the end of camp, each child went home with their own bag of playdough. There are many recipes available online if you'd like to try making your own.

I made a full batch and then divided it into portions to mix in colors and textures. If you choose a different theme, you can easily add glitter, gems, sequins, and more for added fun!

Supplies:

- 3 cups flour
- 3/4 cup table salt
- 4-5 tablespoons cream of tartar
- 3 cups water
- 3 tablespoons vegetable oil
- Food coloring
- Essential oils for a pleasant scent

Instructions:

1. Add the first five ingredients to a large pot and cook over medium heat, stirring continuously.
2. Gradually mix in food coloring, adding a few drops at a time until you achieve your desired hue. I added the color at the end to create different colors in smaller batches as I wanted various colors—just knead it in well. You might want to wear gloves to prevent staining your hands.
3. Continue stirring the mixture over heat until it begins to thicken. Use a silicone spatula to help pull the thickening dough away from the sides and bottom of the pot. Once the mixture forms a ball in the center, remove it from the heat.

4. Transfer the ball onto a lightly floured cutting board or cookie sheet. Carefully knead it until smooth. This is also the time to mix in more food coloring and essential oils, especially if you want to improve the smell of the playdough.
5. Once the playdough has cooled, store it in airtight containers or zip-lock bags to keep it fresh.
6. For construction-themed playdough, consider adding one or more of the following items to small batches:

- Sand
- Organic dirt
- Pea gravel
- Mulch
- Shells

I also set aside some playdough without any of the added materials, so the kids would have a plain option to enjoy and play with.

Snack: Building with Snacks

Supplies:

- One paper plate for each child
- Toothpicks
- Cheese cubes
- Grapes
- Mini marshmallows
- Small apple pieces

I usually set everything out on a tray or table and give each child their own plate. You can encourage them to build anything they can imagine—towers, shapes, animals—whatever comes to mind. It's a great mix of creativity and snacking.

From my experience, the older kids really enjoy the challenge of building something cool. The younger ones? They usually end up munching more than constructing—and that's perfectly fine too!

Let them explore, taste, and have fun. You might be surprised at the edible masterpieces they come up with (or how fast the supplies disappear).

Joy: Day Four

Bible Story: Mark 15:16-32 - The Crucifixion of Jesus

Discussion Questions:

1. Does life ever seem hard? Was there a time when you've faced a challenge or struggle?
2. Is there anything in your life that is painful?
3. Why did Jesus choose to die on the cross?
   This is a great opportunity to share the gospel and discuss themes of sacrifice and redemption.
4. What did Jesus focus on to help Him endure the pain?
   Discuss the thoughts or beliefs that might have given Jesus' strength during His suffering. He may have been thinking of all the people that He was dying for and how His death would change their lives.
5. Who can help you be strong and joyful, even when life gets tough?
   The most important person is Jesus. He knows suffering and pain and can help you overcome whatever you encounter. God also provides people and other sources of support in your life that uplift and encourage you.

Snack: Peanut Butter Banana Quesadillas

Ingredients:

- 1 8-inch tortilla (I chose whole wheat)

- 2 tablespoons peanut butter
- ½ medium banana
- 1 tablespoon semi-sweet chocolate chips

Directions:

1. Spread the peanut butter evenly over the tortilla.
2. Thinly slice the banana and arrange the slices on one half of the tortilla.
3. Sprinkle the chocolate chips over the banana slices, then fold the tortilla in half.
4. Cook the quesadilla in a skillet over medium-low heat until both sides are golden brown and crispy. Enjoy—these were a big hit for our grandkids!

Activity: Joy Toss Game

Supplies:

- 3 paper plates of one color
- 6 paper plates, either white or another color
- Sharpie
- Bean bags (or something similar like small stuffed animal, small pillow)

Instructions:

1. **Prepare the Plates:** On the three paper plates, draw sad or frowning faces. On the other paper plates, write statements that reinforce what was learned in the Bible lessons. Some examples include:

- Joy doesn't come from the things the world offers.
- Joy is in my heart.
- Joy comes from Jesus.
- Joy in the Bible is better than gold.

- Joy comes with confessing.
- God's joy lasts forever.

2. **Set Up the Game:** Lay the paper plates on the floor, either in rows or randomly (they will move around as the game progresses), mixing in the different colored plates. If you wish to prevent the plates from moving, you can tape them down securely. Mark a spot on the floor for the children to stand, adjusting the distance based on their ages, with younger kids standing closer.
3. **Playing the Game:** Explain the goal is to toss the bean bags and try to avoid the sad faces. Each child takes turns tossing the bean bags. As they land on a plate, read the corresponding statement aloud. If they land on a plate with words, encourage them to smile and celebrate, perhaps giving them a treat like a cookie or an Almond Joy® before they sit down. If they land on a sad face plate, frown and let them know that it's okay to feel that way sometimes. Remind them that God wants us to build joy into our lives, even in less-than-ideal situations. They can go to the back of the line and wait for their next turn.
4. **Wrap Up:** Continue playing until all the children have had a turn and received a treat. Use this time to discuss how we can choose joy, even when things don't go our way and reflect on how God guides us in our growth.

Reflections and Award Ceremony

This year, we repurposed some of PaQ's old trophies by creating personalized labels for each child. Each trophy had the child's name and a special recognition, such as "Nicholas Chose Joy." These trophies were awarded to all the kids to celebrate their achievements.

We also recorded the children reciting their Bible verses, which we sent to their parents as a keepsake (as we mentioned earlier in the book).

Peace

Introduction

During our fourth annual Grandkids Camp, I had five little ones in my care—ages 10, 5, 4, 3, and 2. Creating activities that work for such a wide range of ages is definitely a challenge, but I think we pulled it off pretty well overall. This year, I added a few new elements to camp, one of which was inviting my niece, who was almost fifteen at the time, to join us as a junior counselor. She was an incredible help—especially during craft time, meals, and bedtime routines. Her love for Jesus and for the kids really stood out. Our niece didn't just help out; she actively encouraged the children in their lessons and even took the initiative to have them practice their memory verse throughout the day.

We also introduced a new tradition this year—a nightly blessing. Each evening before bed, PaQ took time to individually bless each child, and they were genuinely eager to receive it. We learned about this practice in a class on intentional grandparenting at church, and it really resonated with us. The blessing we chose fit perfectly with our theme and added such a meaningful touch to the end of each day.

Bedtime Blessing

The Lord bless you and keep you;
The Lord make His face to shine upon you,

And be gracious to you;
The Lord lift up His countenance upon you,
And give you PEACE.

Numbers 6:24-26

After getting ready for bed, we had them line up for their blessing from PaQ, and they all waited patiently. Even the ten-year-old seemed to appreciate it and showed no desire to skip it!

Memory Verse: John 14:27

"Peace I leave with you; my peace I give to you. Not as the world gives do I give you. Let not your hearts be troubled, neither let it be afraid."

I enjoy creating actions to help the kids remember the verse, and it's incredible how quickly they pick it up! We recited it every morning at breakfast and throughout the day.

Our song was "Peace Like a River." It was so encouraging to hear the kids request this song before bedtime!

While researching this theme, I discovered several quick games that turned out to be really helpful. We had a rainy day during camp, so we used those extra games to fill the time we would have spent swimming, and it worked out perfectly!

Peace: Day One

I introduced the theme by talking with the kids about how the fruit of the Spirit in our lives shows others what kind of people we are. For this week, we focused on the fruit of the Spirit called *peace*. I explained that having peace means we trust God, even when things get tough. Everyone has hard days or faces challenges, but how we respond in those moments really matters. We can choose to panic, get angry, yell, or stomp our feet—or we can choose to lean on God. He is our ultimate source of peace, and that peace comes only when we submit our lives to Him. Even when things don't go our way, having God's peace helps us stay calm and be there for others when they need support

Bible Lesson: Isaiah 9:6-7 - Jesus is the Prince of Peace

Discussion Questions:

1. Who is the Prince of Peace?
2. What are some other names given to Jesus?

When you trust Jesus with your life, you can truly experience peace. Take a moment and think—what's one thing that makes you feel worried? Remember, Jesus came to bring peace, and one day, there will be no more fighting, sadness, arguing, or anything that makes us afraid. For now, we can hold onto the peace of Jesus inside us, knowing that He has everything under control. How do we get the peace of Jesus inside? This comes through faith in Jesus when we ask Him to forgive us of our sins and submit our lives to Him.

Activity: Noise or Peace

Supplies:

- Noise reduction earmuffs[3]

I borrowed these from one of my children, and they're the same kind used for shooting guns. When I asked to borrow his, our son got a bit worried and thought we might be shooting targets! I had to jokingly reassure him that we wouldn't be doing that until the children are at least twelve years old.

---

[3] Purchase at http://www.amazon.com/dp/B0017YGE8A

Instructions:

Everyone experiences worry sometimes, even parents and grandparents. Children might get nervous about a test, feel anxious about work, or be scared when hearing someone arguing. (Insert things you know your grandchildren fear.) Grandparents, share something you've worried about too.

One great way to handle our worries is through prayer because God can help! In Philippians 4:6-7, we're reminded not to worry but to pray about what troubles us.

Now, let's try something together to help you understand peace. Explain to the children when I say "GO," I want everyone to make as much noise as you can. Wait for my signal! When I raise my hand like this (demonstrate a "stop" hand motion), you need to stop and be quiet. Do you all understand? Okay, ready, set, go! (After a few seconds, or as long as you can handle the noise, raise your hand to signal them to stop.)

All that noise is what it is like for anyone who doesn't know Jesus. There is no peace, only noise and confusion.

When we live for Jesus, we can pray about our worries. Sometimes God brings us peace on the outside, just like when I raised my hand and took away the noise. But it doesn't always happen that way. Sometimes, the things that worry us keep happening! For instance, if you pray about schoolwork, God usually won't cancel school.

When you trust God, you can find peace on the inside, no matter what's happening on the outside. You might pray as Philippians 4 encourages us, sharing your worries with God while also thanking Him—not for the worry, but for His ability to help you through it all, no matter what is happening. When you talk to God in prayer, you'll start to feel some of His peace because you're letting Him take care of your worries.

Now, let me show you what that looks like. We're going to make noise again, but first, we'll give some "peace" to a volunteer, even while everyone is being loud. Pick a volunteer child and put the noise reduction earmuffs on them.

Once the earmuffs are on, it's time for the noise. Ready, Set—GO! (After a few seconds, raise your hand to signal them to stop.)

Now, ask the volunteer, "What did you think? Was that a more peaceful experience, even with everyone making noise and going nuts?" Take turns letting each child try on the earmuffs and experience what it sounds like when everyone is loud.

When you trust God with your worries, sometimes He brings you peace on the outside—just like when we stopped the noise. Other times, He works like the earmuffs, giving you peace on the inside because you're relying on His love and strength, even when the world around you feels chaotic. Just like our verse says, *"Peace I leave with you, my peace I give you,"* His peace is what comforts us from within.

Craft: Cross Craft

Supplies:

- Red paper
- Old magazines
- Pencil
- Glue
- Strong tacky glue
- Wooden frame (similar to a shadow box frame)
- Broken tiles (we saved some from a previous tiling project)

Instructions:

1. **Preparation:** On a piece of wood, draw a wooden cross as a guide. For younger children, use a piece of red paper and draw a cross on it. Then, prepare some old magazines for them to tear up.
2. **Explain the Purpose:** Before you start the project—or even while you're working on it—take a moment to think about what you're creating. The world is broken just like the ripped paper and broken tiles. And just like those pieces need to be put back together, our world does too. Jesus was born to bring peace to our world and put all the broken pieces of our world back together!! God accomplished this through the cross and His Son, Jesus. When God brings His peace into your life, it fills your heart with deep, lasting joy!
3. **Creating the Cross:** You are going to make a cross using all the broken pieces of either tiles or ripped paper. The cross of Jesus is the only way to put the pieces back together and give you true peace in your hearts and lives.
4. **Crafting:** For younger children, you can let them tear up pictures from magazines. Give them either paper with a cross drawn in the middle or a wooden frame. They can glue the ripped pieces onto the outline of the cross to create a beautiful reminder that Jesus brings peace and healing to your life.
5. **Using tiles**: Remember—they can be sharp, so handle them carefully. You can glue the tiles into the shape of a cross, creating a unique piece of art that reminds you of the peace Jesus offers.
6. **Completing:** Once you've finished your project, set it aside to let it dry. After it's dry, you can write a simplified version of John 14:27 at the bottom of your artwork: *"Peace I leave with you; my peace I give you…"*

All of our grandkids used the tiles with our help. The oldest child (age ten) was allowed to use tile nippers to cut some pieces into smaller sizes.

Snack: Fruit and Yogurt Parfait

Supplies:

- Berries
- Yogurt (vanilla or plain)
- Granola
- Clear plastic cups

Instructions:

Allow the children to layer the ingredients, beginning with granola, then yogurt and berries. Continue layering until the cup is full. This is a delightful and healthy snack.

Craft: Gospel Bracelets

Supplies:

- Beads in the following colors: yellow, black, red, white, and green
- String (I recommend stretchy string for easy removal). Supplies may be found at a craft store.

Instructions:

Have the children string the beads in the specified order, explaining the meaning of each color:

1. **Yellow** represents heaven—God created it for us and desires for us to be with Him forever.
2. **Black** symbolizes sin—our sins separate us from God, preventing us from entering heaven.
3. **Red** stands for the blood of Jesus—He died on the cross for our sins, and His blood cleanses us from our sin when we ask for His forgiveness. When we ask His forgiveness, then He washes us clean.

4. **White** signifies being clean—we are made clean by the blood of Jesus when we choose to follow Him.
5. **Green** represents growth—we can grow in our love for Jesus daily through reading the Bible, praying, and attending church.

I printed out cards to send home with the children.[4] I printed just side two with the color explanations and cut them out to put with their items when they went home.

Activity- Magic Show/Testimony

Our grandkids are always thrilled when PaQ pretends to pull a toy out of their ear, calling it magic. They're completely captivated, and PaQ really plays it up for them. Interestingly, PaQ's own journey of faith began at a magic show. When he was eight, his family attended a magic show performance. At the end of the show, the magician revealed that everything he had done that night was an illusion, but Jesus and His miracles were not illusions. The magician went on to share the gospel, and afterward, in the parking lot, PaQ felt compelled to return and pray. His mom and aunt took him back, and it was then that he committed his life to Jesus. We want our grandchildren to hear these important faith stories, so what better way than for PaQ to put on a magic show of his own?

He bought a couple of magic tricks on Amazon, and trust me, they were utterly amazed. Even if your testimony doesn't include magic shows, I would recommend incorporating it into your camp.

The first trick involved changing handkerchiefs to different colors. These can be found quite affordably on Amazon—just search for "magic handkerchiefs." They arrived in primary colors, so we explained that the blue (let's pretend it's black) represents sin, while the red symbolizes how Jesus washes it away. PaQ then asked if the children thought he could transform the colors. He told them he will transform them into green,

---

[4] Purchase at https://www.jeffgossministries.org/salvation-bracelets

symbolizing growth—how once we confess our sins and accept Jesus's sacrifice, we will grow to be more like Him. Then he would change blue into yellow, representing heaven where we can spend eternity with God. He then wowed everyone by changing the colors as he smoothly fed the handkerchiefs through his hand.

The next trick featured paper mouth coils, which he could pull endlessly from his mouth. These can also be found on Amazon under "Magic Mouth Coils." He instructed the kids to tear off a piece of paper, put it in their mouths, and then spit it out. This trick isn't recommended for very young children, as they might accidentally swallow the paper or choke. While they were busy putting a piece of paper in their mouths, he inserted the magic coil and began pulling out paper for quite a while, delighting in their amazed expressions. At the end of the show, he shared the story of the magic show he attended as a child, and how that experience led him to repent of his sins and submit to Jesus Christ as Lord.

Peace: Day Two

Bible Story: Mark 4:35-41 - Jesus Calms a Storm

Discussion Questions:

1. Does this story show that Jesus was human like us? How?
2. What actions of Jesus in this passage reveal He was God?
3. How did the disciples feel during the storm? Are you afraid of storms? Afraid of anything else?
4. What was Jesus doing while the storm raged? What did Jesus do when He woke up?
5. Did the storm obey Him? What did this show about Jesus?
6. What did Jesus say to calm the storm?
7. Do you think the disciples had a greater faith in Jesus after this?

Jesus showed that He is God by calming the storm. He was not just human like us; He was and is all powerful. He is worthy of our faith in Him.

Game: Storm and Peace

This game can be fun for kids as young as 4, though younger children—like 2-year-olds—might have trouble understanding the rules. Your little ones (like our grandson) might get upset if their flag is taken, even though that's part of the game. It works well outdoors, but if that's not possible, you can play in the largest room available in your home—just be sure to establish clear boundaries.

Supplies:

- A flag for each child (we used bandanas in two different colors)
- If you have enough kids, you can create teams.

Instructions:

1. **Team Setup**: Divide the children into two teams using the different-colored flags or bandanas. If playing outside, establish boundaries and set up two safe zones opposite each other for each team.
2. **Flag Placement**: Each child should tuck a flag into their waistband, so it hangs down one leg or in the back. It should be easily accessible for grabbing, similar to flag football.
3. **Game Play**: When you shout "Storm," both teams rush toward each other, aiming to pull out the other players' flags while protecting their own. If a player loses their flag, they sit out on the side.
4. **Safe Zones**: If a player reaches the opposite safe zone, they are safe and can no longer lose their flag or take anyone else's.
5. **Timing**: Let the game continue for about 15-30 seconds, depending on your space and number of children.
6. **Freezing the Game**: When you say "PEACE," everyone must freeze and the game pauses. Alternate between "Storm" and "PEACE."

Important Rules:

- Players can only grab flags, not hold onto other players.
- To protect their flags, players can only run away; they cannot hold their flags or push others.
- Demonstrate what's allowed and what's not before starting. You can have grandparents act as referees or participate.

Play as many rounds as the children would like.

Ending the Game:

After you finish playing, have a seat and take a moment to think about the game. Explain it's called "Storm and Peace." Just like you felt the chaos during the storm part of the game, real life can sometimes feel stormy too. But when you froze during "PEACE," you experienced a moment of calm.

One day, Jesus will come back and bring complete peace. He'll stop all the storms, all the fights, and all the worries. If you follow Him, you won't have anything to be afraid of, because He'll take away all the bad things in the world. Everything will be peaceful. Doesn't that sound amazing?

Even though we live in a world that has problems and challenges, you can still find peace in God. When you feel afraid or worried, you can pray, saying something like: "God, no matter what happens, I'm going to trust You, because I know You love me and care for me."

Remember, God's peace can fill your heart—just like you felt safe in the game's safe zone or how Jesus calmed the storm for His disciples. Anytime you feel scared or unsure, talk to God. He's always there to bring you comfort.

Craft: Jesus Calms the Storm

Supplies:

- Paper plates
- Scissors
- Crayons or markers
- White cardstock paper
- Drinking straws
- Tape

Instructions:

1. **Prepare the Plates**: Cut the paper plates in half, giving each child one half.
2. **Create the Waves**: With the straight edge of the plate at the top, have the children draw high waves across the bottom of the plate and color in their boat (the paper plate).
3. **Make the Sail**: Cut a square sail from the white cardstock. Write the Bible verse for the week on the sail, such as "Jesus calms the storm" or "Peace, be still." Encourage the children to choose any theme-related verse they want for their sail.
4. **Attach the Sail**: Tape the straw onto the back of the plate to serve as a mast, then attach the sail to the straw.
5. **Display**: Let the children show their creations and retell the story using their boat as a prop!

Craft: Paint Peace Signs

I found some charming wooden signs that say "PEACE" at the dollar store, and they make a great craft for kids. Keep an eye out for similar peace-themed crafts to incorporate into your activities.

Instructions:

1. **Painting the Signs**: Let the kids paint the wooden peace signs however they like, encouraging their creativity and personal expression.
2. **Cleanup Tip**: To make cleanup easier, pick up a few disposable tablecloths from the dollar store. Spread them on the table before painting, and when the kids are done, simply fold up the tablecloth with all the mess inside and throw it away.

Snack: Cream Wafer Cookies

I made one of my grandkids' favorite cookies, cream wafers, and he was eager to help me prepare them. It was a fantastic way to get him (and the other grandchildren) involved in baking—especially since he found it fun and knew he'd get to enjoy the results. I had him help with simple tasks like stirring and pouring ingredients into the bowl.

Cream Wafer Recipe from Lynn Stieber:

Ingredients:

Filling (I sometimes double this because it's so delicious.):

- ¼ cup soft butter
- ¾ cup sifted powdered sugar
- 1 egg yolk
- 1 teaspoon vanilla extract
- Food coloring (optional)

Cookies:

- 1 cup butter or margarine
- ⅓ cup whipping cream
- 2 cups flour
- Sugar (for coating)

Directions:

1. **Prepare the Cookie Dough**: In a bowl, mix the butter, whipping cream, and flour until thoroughly combined. Chill the dough for 1 hour.
2. **Preheat the Oven**: Set your oven to 375°F (190°C).
3. **Roll Out the Dough**: On a lightly floured surface, roll the dough to about 1/8 inch thick. Cut into 1½-inch rounds using a small biscuit cutter.
4. **Sugar Coating**: Transfer the cookie rounds to a bowl with sugar and coat both sides.
5. **Prepare for Baking**: Place the cookies on an ungreased baking sheet. Prick each cookie in 3-4 places with a fork.
6. **Bake**: Bake for 9-10 minutes or until the cookies are slightly puffy.
7. **Make the Filling**: In a bowl, blend the soft butter, powdered sugar, egg yolk, and vanilla until smooth. Tint with food coloring if desired.
8. **Assemble**: Once cooled, put two cookies together with the filling.

This recipe makes about 5 dozen cookies, perfect for sharing and enjoying together!

Peace: Day Three

Bible Lesson: Matthew 6:25-34 – Do Not Worry

Discussion questions (to be asked before reading the Bible passage):

1. Do you ever worry if the sun will rise tomorrow?
2. Do you ever worry that your heart will forget how to keep pumping blood?

3. Do you ever worry that a chair might not hold you when you sit down?
4. Why don't you worry about these things?
5. What other things don't cause you to worry?
6. What kinds of things do you tend to worry about?
7. Can you name specific worries you have?
8. Why do these worries affect you? What are you afraid might happen?
9. How do the things you worry about differ from the things you don't worry about?
10. Do you think God worries?
11. Do you think He wants us to worry?

Background Information Before the Reading:

Tell the story and background in your own words. Imagine yourself living in the time of Jesus. You would have known that He was a rabbi—a Jewish teacher. Like other rabbis, He had followers who were His students. These followers were called disciples. But Jesus was different from the other rabbis you might have heard of. He performed miracles and spoke with an authority that made Him stand out. He did so many incredible things and taught so many important lessons that John, one of His disciples, once said, *"I suppose that if all the other things Jesus did were written down, the whole world could not contain the books"* (John 21:25).

One of Jesus's most well-known teachings is the Sermon on the Mount (Matthew 5:1–6:34). If you had been there, you would have heard Him talk about how to live a life that pleases God. He covered many parts of everyday life and explained how to follow God's will in a deeper way. Do you remember what God gave Moses on the mountain? He gave the Ten Commandments—the rules people followed to live God's way before Jesus came.

Jesus's teachings in the Sermon on the Mount are commandments from the New Testament. In them, Jesus shows you how to follow God's rules in practical, everyday ways. When you choose to submit your life to Jesus, become His disciple, and truly follow Him, these teachings become your guidelines for how to live.

When you follow God's ways and obey His Word, something happens—the result is fruit in your life. Right now, you're learning about peace, which is one of the fruits of the Spirit. In the few verses from today's lesson, Jesus says, **"Do not worry"** five times.

As I read this, every time you hear the words **"Do not worry"** or something similar, start counting out loud. Let's see if you can find all five.

Read Matthew 6:25-34.

Discussion Questions:

1. What does Jesus tell you not to worry about in the first verse? Our life, what we eat or drink, our body, and what we wear - v. 25. That sounds like everything, doesn't it?
2. What does Jesus tell you to be like? The birds in the air - v. 26. Birds don't worry about what to eat because God feeds them.
3. Why does it matter to you that God feeds the birds? Because you are more valuable to God than birds - v. 26.
4. In verse 27 Jesus asks, "Who of you by worrying can add a single hour to his life?" What's the answer? No one.
5. What do flowers not worry about? How beautiful they look - v. 28.
6. What are we missing when we worry? Faith - v. 30. You can ask God to give you faith. It is a gift from Him to believe in Jesus and to help you to not worry.
7. What does God our Father know? He knows what we need. — v. 32.

Activity: Planting

Supplies:

- Flower seeds
- Small pots or cups
- Soil

Instructions:

Add soil to the pots or cups and place seeds on top. Add additional soil if needed. As you do this, you can tell the children: A seed can't grow into something beautiful unless it's planted in soil, watered, and given sunlight. The same is true for you. If you want to grow to be more like Jesus, you need to be "planted," "watered," and receive "sunlight" too. You do that by reading the Bible, praying, and spending time with other followers of Jesus.

Marigolds are a great choice because they're simple and quick to grow. So, enjoy the process—get your hands in the soil and have fun planting together!

Game: Thumbs Up or Down

Instructions:

Gather the children and explain the game as follows:

When I say a word, you'll show me how it makes you feel. If the word reminds you of peace, give me a thumbs up and a big smile. But if the word does not remind you of peace, give me a thumbs down and a frown.

- Happy
- Sad
- Angry
- Calm
- Stars

- River
- Hugs
- Hitting
- Sharing
- Taking turns
- Rainbow
- Tornado
- Being selfish
- Saying mean words
- A compliment
- Cleaning up
- Making a mess

Activity: Bean Bag Toss Game

Supplies:

- Bean bags
- 10-15 printed pictures that represent either peace or not peace (you can find images in magazines, such as lakes, animals, sunsets, sport events, traffic jams, a cross, the empty tomb, a Bible verse, a song title, someone praying, etc.)

Purpose:

The peace that the world offers is so different from God's peace.

Instructions:

1. **Setup:** Print and display the pictures. Lay them out on the floor after showing them to the children. Some should depict peaceful scenes that the world would consider peaceful, while others show chaotic or unpeaceful situations, and there should be some that represent God's peace.

2. **Game Instructions:** Have the children take turns tossing bean bags at the pictures. After each toss, ask: Does this picture show God's peace or the world's idea of peace? Why or why not?
3. **Discussion:** Do you think you could find peace in all the pictures? How? Jesus promised His disciples peace—not the kind of peace the world offers, but God's true peace. When you are a follower of Jesus, you can have His peace no matter the circumstances.

Activity: Blindfold Obstacle Course

Purpose:

This activity teaches children to trust God and follow Him, even when they don't understand the reasons behind their journey.

Instructions:

1. **Setup:**
    a. Create a simple obstacle course using chairs, blocks, tape on the floor, and any safe furniture for crawling over, under, or around.
    b. Use bandanas from the previous Storm and Peace game as blindfolds.
2. **Demonstration:**
    a. Let the children walk through the obstacle course without blindfolds first.
    b. After they finish, ask them if it was easy or hard (they'll likely say "easy").
    c. Ask if they think it will be easy to navigate the course while blindfolded and what it would be like to have someone guide them.
3. **Blindfold Activity:**
    a. Pair up the children. One child will be blindfolded while the other guides them through the obstacle course by holding hands or touching their shoulders.

   b. Remind them not to talk, just to guide gently.
   c. Stay close and encourage them with phrases like "Good job!" as they navigate.
   d. Switch so they can all have a turn being blindfolded and being the guide.

4. **Discussion:**
   a. After everyone has had a turn, gather the children to discuss their experiences.
   b. Relate their blindfolded navigation to trusting God: just as they had to trust their partner, they need to trust God during difficult times.
   c. Emphasize that God sees what we cannot and will lead us through challenges, even when we don't understand. Just like you maybe didn't understand where your guide was leading you because you couldn't see what your guide could see.
   d. Trusting in God gives us peace.

5. **Adaptation:**
   a. Instead of physically guiding the blindfolded child, have the partner give verbal instructions. This will help the blindfolded child learn to listen carefully, similar to how we must listen to Jesus.
   b. Discuss how challenging it can be to give clear instructions, reinforcing the idea that we should let Jesus guide us, as He knows the way better than we do.

Wrap up:

Learning to trust God in all circumstances begins with trusting God for salvation. This means acknowledging Him as your only source of forgiveness of your sin and for eternal life through Jesus Christ. This is a gift from God and cannot be earned through your good works. You must repent and turn from your sin, trusting in God's promise to forgive you.

When you have this trust in God for your greatest need, then trusting Him in your daily challenges is possible.

Craft: Peace wreath

Introduction:

Begin the craft by explaining to the children that God created all people, loves each one of us, and wants everyone to know Him. Tell them that He has called you—and all of us—to make disciples of every nation, tribe, and language. True peace is found in following Jesus and becoming His disciple.

Point out that each nation is represented by a different flag, and people come in many different skin colors. Ask the children, "Does God love all the nations equally?" Then remind them that the answer is yes—because He created them all.

Encourage the children to show God's love and strive to live in peace with others, no matter how different someone may seem. Remind them that even though some countries are experiencing conflict or war, God still wants everyone to experience the peace that comes through Jesus. Let them know that even in the midst of hardship, people can still find true peace in Him

Since you've received Christ's peace freely, remind the children that we're called to share that peace freely with others as well.

This is a great time to teach them the song "Jesus Loves the Little Children of the World."

Supplies:

- Wreath Frame: Make one from poster board, cardboard, or use a foam wreath—feel free to get creative!
- Tacky Glue: Tacky glue works best to secure the handprints onto the wreath.

- Printed Flags from various countries or different colored paper for each child: Use the colors from the song—red, yellow, black, white, but add brown, tan, and any other skin color you would like.
- Pencil
- Scissors

Instructions:

If you are using flags, have the children trace their hands on the back of each flag to represent different people groups. If you are using colors, have them trace their hands on different colors of paper. Younger children may need help tracing their hands. Cut out the hand shapes and have the children attach them to the wreath using glue. Be sure they use a variety of colors or flags to represent many different nations.

Peace: Day Four

Bible Lesson: II Thessalonians 3:16

This verse is also a blessing and a great way to close the week. "*Now may the Lord of peace Himself give you peace at all times in every way. The Lord be with you all*"

Activity: Instruments

Supplies:

- Wooden spoons
- Pots, pan, or metal bowls

This activity works well for younger children, and even older ones—like ten-year-olds—will enjoy the chance to bang on pots and pans!

Start by playing soft music in the background. When you're ready, tell them to bang on their pots and sing loudly when you say "Go," and to stop when you say "Stop." Let them enjoy making noise for a while.

When you're finished, collect the instruments and have everyone sit together to listen quietly to the music.

Afterward, ask each child which part—making noise or listening to the calm music—felt more peaceful. Use that moment to talk with them about how the quiet music is like the peace that God gives. Remind them that trusting God and knowing He's always with us brings peace, no matter what's going on around us.

Reflections

The last day is a great opportunity to wrap up any unfinished crafts or activities. We usually have the children pack up their belongings, and once they're done, they get to watch a show or movie—a special treat we don't typically offer during the week. This also gives us time to organize and pack the rest of their things.

One month after camp this year, our daughter shared that our youngest grandson, who was two and a half at the time, walked up to his brother, placed his hand on his shoulder, and said, "I give you a blessing. The Lord bless you, lift up His countenance, and give you peace." Even though he didn't remember it all, it was so encouraging to see him wanting to share this blessing with his older brother. Later, he even tried to give a blessing to some friends who visited. While he didn't remember the entire blessing perfectly, he did a great job with it and was eager to share blessings with others! When their parents share stories like this, it makes all the time, effort and exhaustion worthwhile as we invest in their lives.

Patience

Introduction

This year, we decided to invite our oldest god-grandson at a different time and focus the activities on the younger kids. We had children aged 6, 5, 4, 3, and 2 attending this year. As they grow, they can start helping out more. We encouraged them to clean up after meals by taking their plates to the kitchen, which they enjoyed— even the two-year-old wanted to do it herself! However, when I instructed her to scrape the food into the trash, she accidentally tossed her plate and spoon in the trash too. We worked through the idea of scraping food into the trash together. They can also fill their own water bottles and assist the younger ones with theirs, pick up their clothes, and put their toys where they belong.

Typically, we gather all the families together and then the children stay for about four days before we either take them home or meet halfway with their parents. This year, we decided to change things up and took the kids down to the lake in the morning so they arrived around nap time. They had a late breakfast before leaving home and ate an early lunch on the way, which meant they needed a snack before their naps. The first day was mostly about setting up, organizing, and introducing the theme of patience. We didn't have much time since bedtime was around seven for most of the kids. After they arrived and took their naps, we managed to cover the rules, introduce the theme, and share the song, which they really enjoyed. If you have a long drive, it's a great opportunity to start discussing this year's theme, Bible verse, and practice patience in the car as you kick off Grandkids Camp.

This year's theme will not only challenge the children but also the grandparents. We all need to practice patience, as things may not always go as planned or happen as quickly as we'd like. We might also need to introduce new or different activities (see the extra activities at the end of the chapter).

Memory Verse: Ephesians 4:2

"...with all humility and gentleness, with patience, bearing with one another in love."

This is a verse we can reference throughout the day, especially when the kids are struggling with kindness or patience toward each other. I enjoy reminding them of the verse during our various activities, and they love to remind their grandparents to be patient as well!

Our song this year was "Have Patience," by His and Hernandez Music, which you can find on YouTube,[5] if you're not familiar with the words or tune. I kept it simple: We watched the YouTube video together and then continued singing the song "Have Patience" ourselves.

By the end of the week, we had all learned the chorus and were singing it enthusiastically. Even on the first day, as we walked to the water, the 2-year-old proudly led the line and the 6-year-old spontaneously started singing the song.

As your group of kids gets older, you'll probably notice that some no longer need naps, while others still depend on them to make it through the day. For the non-nappers, you can introduce a lesson in patience by having

---

[5] "Have Patience, https://www.youtube.com/watch?v=iL1BRPEjMZA

them work on a puzzle throughout the week. I recommend setting up a designated space on the first day—maybe a corner of the room or an extra card table—where the puzzle can stay undisturbed.

Choose one that's challenging enough to keep them engaged, but not so hard that they get discouraged and give up. You might want to have a few simpler puzzles available too, so they can complete one or two each day. I had a box with 4 puzzles—32, 72, and 100 pieces—and they finished them way faster than I expected! Next time, I'll be sure to bring at least a 200-piece puzzle. I honestly didn't realize how good they already were at puzzles!

Here are some great books for the kids to enjoy during naptime or as bedtime stories. You can find these titles about patience on Amazon or at your local library. It's always a good idea to ask the librarian for suggestions, but I recommend reading the books first to ensure they're appropriate for your grandchildren.

Here are a couple we chose this year.

- *Llama Llama Red Pajama* by Anna Dewdney (They loved this one and asked me to read it multiple times.)
- *Waiting for Wings* by Lois Ehlert
- *Bob & Larry in the Case of the Missing Patience* by Karen Poth (This is an early reader book, so the six-year-old was able to read it to the younger kids.)

After dinner on, I shared my testimony with the children about how I came to know Jesus at the age of eight while attending summer camp. I told them it was the first time I understood that not following Jesus would lead me to spend eternity in hell. I didn't want that, so I confessed my sins and turned to follow Jesus. It took many more years for me to fully grasp what that meant. I explained to the children that our sin separates us from God, and because of this separation, we deserve hell. However, God loves us so much that He sent His Son to die for us and take the punishment we deserve. Because of this, we don't have to face hell if we confess our sin and trust in Jesus. There's nothing we can do to save ourselves, but Jesus has already done that for us. God has patience with us, and He is our source of patience toward others.

Our granddaughter wore her gospel bracelet from last year, which provided a great opportunity to share the gospel with the kids by explaining the meaning of each color.

Patience: Day One

Start by reviewing the Grandkids' Camp rules with the children. Some of the kids remembered the rules from last year, so we began by inviting them to share what they recalled. They always enjoy the first rule—it gets a laugh every time: **No Parents!**

If they're old enough, consider creating a chore chart. Since they'll be responsible for various tasks throughout the week, it's helpful to explain the importance of doing chores promptly and without complaining.

Next, you'll introduce the theme—**Patience**. I like to explain it as the ability to accept or tolerate delays, challenges, or discomfort without getting upset or angry. You can tell the kids that it means staying calm in difficult situations—whether they're waiting for something, dealing with something annoying, or helping someone who's having a hard time understanding. Patience means not losing your cool, even when it feels like you've been waiting forever.

God is incredibly patient with us. Even when we sin—sometimes the same sin over and over—He doesn't give up on us. Instead, in His patience and love, He forgives us when we confess our sin and turn away from it.

Start to learn the Bible verse by saying it several times.

Then set up the TV or computer screen to show the *Have Patience* video with Herber the Snail. Once they have seen the video, you can sing the chorus with the children to help them learn it.

Craft: Play Doh® or Clay Snails

Supplies:

- Play Doh® or modeling clay (we used white air-dry clay)
- Paint brushes
- Paint

These adorable snails are a fun and creative way to encourage kids to practice patience. Once they're finished, the snails can be displayed throughout the week as a gentle visual reminder.

Instructions:

1. Begin by rolling out two clay "snakes"—one shorter and one longer but not too skinny.
2. Take the longer piece, flatten it slightly, then roll it into a spiral.
3. Place this spiral on top of the shorter piece, pressing them together firmly to ensure they stick. This step is important—if they don't bond well, you might need to use glue later. (We ran into this problem with a couple of the snails.)
4. You can also add eyes and antennae if you have time. We didn't get to that part, since our clay needed a couple of days to dry.
5. After they are completely dry, then they can be painted.

Bible Lesson: Genesis 17:1-6, 17—Abraham and Sarah

Read Genesis 17:1-6, 17 or from *The Jesus Storybook Bible*, the story titled "Son of Laughter," or read it from both sources.

After sharing the story, engage the children with some questions. This can be especially entertaining, since their perception of age is often quite different. I loved when my grandson said his dad was 60, which was older than me at the time, and that his mom was 25, when she was actually over 30!

Discussion:

1. How old do you think Abraham and Sarah were?
2. Is 35 too old to have a baby? What about 55? Or even 75?
3. Sometimes, God asks us to wait—even when He's already promised us something good. God promised that Abraham would be the father of many people, but as he grew older, he and his wife Sarah still didn't have any children. They believed what God had said, but it was hard to understand how the promise would come true. How could Abraham be a father without any kids?
4. Did they trust God for a child? Even though the wait was long and hard, Abraham and Sarah chose to trust God. Their patience wasn't perfect—they made some mistakes and tried to take control at times—but God was still faithful. He forgave them, and in His perfect timing, He kept His promise.

Reflections:

We can use this story to help kids understand that sometimes both God and parents ask us to wait for good reasons. It's not always easy—we might feel like rushing ahead or trying to make things happen on our own. But real patience means trusting without complaining, even when it's hard. And when we wait well, the blessings that come afterward feel even more special.

God also fulfilled another promise to Abraham and his people, which took much longer than for Sarah to become pregnant. He sent Jesus hundreds of years later to redeem all people through His sacrifice on the cross.

Craft: Nightlight

Supplies:

- Small clear plastic cups (one per child)
- Black or blue acrylic paint
- Star stickers any size and shape (you may also offer other shapes of stickers if they prefer something unique, like hearts, flowers etc.)
- Sponges or brush
- Battery-operated tea light candle (one per child)

This nightlight serves as a reminder for the children to be patient, just like Abraham and Sarah, and to trust that God will be faithful to His promises. Just as He promised Abraham many descendants like the stars in the sky, this craft encourages them to pray and give thanks for His promises.

Instructions:

1. Begin by protecting the table from messes.
2. Have the kids stick the star stickers all over their plastic cups.
3. Then, using the sponge or brush, let them paint the entire outside of the cup, including over the stars.
4. Allow the paint to dry. While they wait, this could be a great opportunity for another craft or a snack.
5. Once the cups are dry, have the children carefully remove all the stickers. (We had a hard time removing some stickers because there was too much paint applied.)
6. Place the battery candle underneath each cup, turn it on, and then dim the lights to reveal the beautiful stars shining through their nightlights. They can place these in their rooms to enjoy each night during camp.

Note: Allow plenty of time for the paint to dry completely as it may take a full day.

Craft: Glitter Name

Supplies:

- Black or blue paper
- Glue or glue stick (liquid glue is best)
- Star glitter or any glitter will work

Instructions:

1. Have your grandchildren write their names on the black or blue paper using glue. For younger ones, you can write the names for them.
2. Next, sprinkle glitter on top. Let the artwork dry before shaking off the excess glitter.
3. Encourage them to embellish their names with star stickers or draw stars using light-colored crayons.
4. For an extra creative touch, gather various colors of glitter and have them draw stars, apply glue, and sprinkle different colors on top.

Snack: Star-Shaped Food

Supplies:

- Meats and cheeses
- Ingredients for peanut butter and jelly sandwiches
- Fruit that can be sliced thin (melons work well)
- Star-shaped cookie cutters in various sizes

Use the star-shaped cookie cutters to cut meats, cheeses, and peanut butter and jelly sandwiches into fun star shapes. If you have smaller cutters, you can also make star-shaped slices of fruit. Your grandkids will enjoy the hands-on experience of cutting their own meats, cheeses, sandwiches, and fruit into stars!

Activity: Fishing

Teaching your grandkids to fish is a great way to instill patience, as they learn to wait for a fish to bite. They'll also learn to wait their turn if there aren't enough fishing rods. You might need to help them put a worm on the hook or take a fish off, which gives them more opportunities to practice patience.

Naptime

With young grandchildren—some who still nap and others who don't—we always set aside this time for those who don't nap as quiet time for reading or playing calmly. I've found that this unstructured time really encourages creativity as they come up with their own ways to stay entertained. Be sure to have a variety of options ready, like books, toys, and simple games. During this time, they begin to learn the value of waiting patiently for the napping children to wake up. They can also help out with whatever you're working on, whether it's tidying up or getting ready for the next activity.

Activity: Patience Treats

After naps, I kicked off a fun activity about an hour before dinner called *Patience Treats*. Choose small treats your grandkids enjoy—like Skittles, Swedish Fish, M&Ms, gummy bears, or fruit snacks. Give each child two small bowls or cups: one with a single treat and the other filled with a handful of the same treat. Offer the treat before dinner but let them know they have a choice. You can explain that they can either eat the single treat now or wait patiently until after dinner for the bigger portion.

This concept can be a little tricky for younger kids, so I try to explain it clearly and gently to avoid any frustration. I was honestly impressed the first time we tried this—everyone managed to wait until after dinner for the bigger reward!

If your grandchild chooses to wait, set the larger bowl aside and keep the single treat visible until dinner is finished in case they change their mind. During the meal, talk with them about the choices they made. You can ask whether it was easy or hard to wait, did they have patience, and what helped them decide.

After dinner, give the full bowl of treats to those who waited patiently, and be sure to praise them for their patience. I always remind my grandkids that while waiting can sometimes come with a reward, the real goal is learning to be patient even when there isn't one.

Movie:

Veggie Tales: Abe and the Amazing Promise

I borrowed this movie from my daughter, and it's a great choice for teaching kids about patience as a godly character trait. Any age-appropriate film that emphasizes patience as a godly virtue would be a fun addition to your movie time. To make it special, prepare some popcorn or let the kids enjoy their treats while watching the movie together!

Patience: Day Two

Bible Story: Genesis 37:23-24, 28, 38:1-2, and 45:4-5—Joseph

Read "The Forgiving Prince" from *The Jesus Storybook Bible*, or Genesis 37:23-24, 28, 38:1-2, and 45:4-5. *The Message Bible* is also a great translation to use.

Discussion Questions:

1. Was Joseph scared or angry with his brothers for what they did? No, he chose to trust and wait patiently for God to act.
2. Did Joseph maintain his faith in God while he was waiting after being sold into slavery? Yes, he worked diligently and kept a positive attitude during his time in Egypt.

3. Did Joseph continue to trust God while he was in jail? Absolutely.
4. How was Joseph rewarded for his patient trust in God? He formed a friendship with the king, and through this relationship, God provided for his father and brothers. When we trust God during our waiting periods, we give Him the opportunity to work things out for us.
5. Did Joseph forgive his brothers? Yes, he did. Just as God forgives us through Jesus, we should also forgive others.

You can further discuss how this story points to Jesus, who was unjustly condemned like Joseph. Just as Joseph was eventually placed in a position to save his family from famine, Jesus was condemned and died so that you could be free from your debt of sin.

Craft: Coat of many colors

Supplies:

- Simple shirt drawn on a white piece of paper—1 per child
- Coloring items can include markers, crayons, yard sale label dots, or bingo dot blotters. I like to offer a variety of colors, and since I already had these supplies on hand, I let the kids choose. They all ended up picking the bingo dot blotters.

Instructions:

1. Distribute a paper shirt to each child.
2. Place all the coloring options in the center of the table.
3. If using bingo dot blotters, make sure to protect the table by placing something underneath their paper.
4. Remind the kids to apply the bingo dots gently, avoiding too much pressure, as new blotters can splatter ink if pressed too hard.

Activity/Game: Joseph where is your coat?

Here is a playful twist to the classic "Doggy, Doggy, Where's Your Bone?" game, and we turned it into "Joseph, Joseph, where is your coat (of many colors)?" You'll choose one child to play Joseph. Have them sit in front of the group with their back turned and eyes closed. Place "Joseph's coat"—either a piece of fabric or the craft they made earlier—behind them. Then, pick another child to quietly sneak up, take the coat, and return to their seat, hiding it behind their back.

Once everyone is seated, lead the kids in chanting, "Joseph, Joseph, where's your coat? Somebody took it, guess who?" Joseph then tries to guess who took the coat. If they guess correctly, they get another turn; if not, they switch places with the child who took it. You can also give them two or three guesses, depending on the age group.

Our grandkids absolutely loved this game! It's simple enough that they can easily play during any downtime.

Snack: Joseph's Coat of Many Colors Snack[6]

Supplies:

- Sugar wafer cookies
- Mini chocolate chips
- Red decorating gel (in a tube)
- Crème-filled cookies (like Oreos; you can use a store-brand with vanilla and chocolate)
- Rainbow-colored fruit roll-ups

Instructions:

1. Give each of your grandchildren a plate.
2. For the head, open one crème-filled cookie, using the side with the cream intact.

[6] From "Joseph's Coat of Many Colors Snack," by Kerry Black, How to Homeschool My Child, (https://howtohomeschoolmychild.com/joseph-coat-of-many-colors-craft-snack/). Reprinted with permission. Permission granted by author on March 24, 2025.

3. Add mini chocolate chips for the eyes and use the red decorating gel to draw a mouth.
4. Below the head, place two wafer cookies for the body.
5. Break one of the wafer cookies in half to create the arms.
6. Finally, drape the fruit roll-ups over the arms and body to make a colorful coat of many colors.
7. Once they are finished, let them enjoy their snack.

Outside activities: Hunting for Treasures Requires Patience

Supplies:

- Colorful glass rocks/gems (available at dollar stores, Wal-Mart, or other local discount stores; I bought several bags in different colors.)

We took a boat ride to a local state park beach for a picnic, but you can choose any park, playground, or even your backyard. While the kids are playing, or if you walk ahead, sneak off to another area of the beach, playground, or outdoor space to scatter the "gems." Once they're spread out, invite the children to come and search for the colorful treasures. You might find other kids wanting to join in if you are at a public location, so it's a great opportunity to practice patience and share the love of Jesus by including them. After our grandchildren finished collecting gems, it was amusing to see even adults at the beach getting in on the fun and picking up gems!

After-Dinner activity: Pass the Parcel

Supplies:

- Small prizes (like M&Ms or other individually wrapped treats) for each child
- A box to hold the prizes
- Wrapping paper in at least two different colors

Instructions:

1. In advance of camp, place the small prize inside the box and wrap it in multiple layers of paper—make sure to use at least as many layers as there are children to keep the excitement alive.
2. Have the children form a circle and take turns unwrapping a layer.
3. After the first child removes one layer, they pass the parcel to the next child, and this continues until everyone has had a turn. If some children get extra turns, it adds to the challenge of being patient as they uncover the prize inside.
4. Once they reach the treat, remind them that everyone demonstrated patience, and they can all share the goodies. The anticipation of what's inside will keep their excitement high! As they enjoy their snacks, take a moment to discuss who showed patience and whether the wait was worth it.

Patience: Day Three

Bible Story: Deuteronomy 29:2-5—God's Example of Patience with the Israelites

Introduction:

This lesson is where we see how God demonstrated immense patience with the Israelites, particularly through the story of Moses. These stories vividly illustrate Moses' journey with the Israelites. If it's challenging to read all three in one sitting, consider breaking them up—one at breakfast, one at lunch, and one at dinner. This approach allows for ongoing discussions about God's patience. After each story, ask how God exhibited patience with the Israelites and how He shows patience with us today.

Read Deuteronomy 29:2-5 and from *The Jesus Storybook Bible* - "God to the Rescue!", "God Makes a Way," and "Ten Ways to be Perfect."

Discussion Questions:

1. How many years did God lead Moses and His people through the wilderness toward the Promised Land? Forty years, which is a long time.
2. Did God's people ever doubt Him? Yes.
3. Did they complain or feel like giving up? Absolutely.
4. Yet through it all, why did God continue to show patience and forgiveness? He listened to their cries time and again, sustaining them with manna, water from rocks, and miraculous signs of His goodness. All along, God sought true reconciliation with Israel—and with us. He kept offering opportunities for repentance and restoration, demonstrating His steadfast grace.
5. Do you ever find yourself doubting God, complaining, or feeling like giving up? Remember that God's heart is tender, and He understands our struggles with patience and endurance. He is patient with us when we sin over and over by grumbling and complaining like the Israelites or sin in any other way. He is always there with exactly what we need, right when we need it.
6. When we understand the patience God has shown us, how should we respond? We know that His heart is tender and patient. He understands our struggles and responds with patient endurance. Even when we sin—grumbling like the Israelites—He provides exactly what we need at the exact moment we need it.

Reflection:

Recognizing God's remarkable patience should shape our response: we're called to reflect His character. When God offers grace, humility, and second chances, we should extend that same grace to others. By practicing patience ourselves, we mirror His mercy and character in our own lives.

Craft/Activity: Baking Cookies or Muffins—A Lesson in Patience

Baking cookies or muffins is a great way to teach patience, especially since the Israelites longed for food during their journey. As you bake, you'll experience the importance of waiting— whether it's for your turn to stir, mix, or for the oven to preheat.

Consider what might happen if we rushed the process. What if we didn't mix the ingredients thoroughly? Or what if we took the cookies or muffins out of the oven too soon because we weren't patient and couldn't wait? The results wouldn't be as delicious!

To make this experience more engaging, have the children gather around the table and take turns. We had the children pass the bowl around so they could each have a turn stirring and adding ingredients to the bowl. This not only fosters patience but also makes the baking process fun and collaborative!

Snack: Pineapple

For a tasty snack, cut a whole pineapple! This activity will teach about patience as the children wait to enjoy it together.

Supplies:

- Whole pineapple
- Knife
- Bowl for the pineapple chunks
- Large cutting board

Instructions:

Begin by cutting the pineapple while the children watch. As you work, ask them if they think it takes a long time to cut a pineapple. Use this moment to discuss patience—emphasizing how it requires patience to wait to eat the pineapple together. Once it's all cut up, everyone can enjoy the delicious fruit as a reward for their patience.

Craft: Patient Pineapples

Supplies:

- Brown paper bags (one per child) or mini brown paper bags
- Yellow paint or yellow paint markers
- Recycled plastic grocery bags, newspaper, tissue paper, or any scrap paper for stuffing
- Glue
- Packing tape (works best for this activity) or twine.

Instructions:

1. **Create the Leaves:** Cut out strips in the top of the paper bag and color or paint them green.
2. **Decorate the Pineapple:** Have the children paint or color the brown paper bags with yellow to represent the pineapple's exterior.
3. **Fill the Pineapple:** Use plastic or paper bags, tissue paper or the pre-cut strips of newspaper, to fill the bottom of the brown paper bag. Remind the children to lightly ball the stuffing; if they ball them too tightly, you'll need more to fill the bag.
4. **Assemble:** Gather the top of the bag and tape or tie it closed.

After the pineapples are complete, share with the children that their creations symbolize patience, just like waiting for the delicious pineapple snack!

Patience: Day Four

We planned an excursion to an amusement park. You can plan a trip to any local activity that would require a little bit of a drive. During breakfast, take a moment to go over the verse and remind everyone that today will call for plenty of patience. Patience will be important as we drive to our destination, since it will take some time to arrive. We'll need to practice patience while waiting in line for rides or activities as well. Since this was a full-day event, we didn't schedule any stories or additional activities for the day.

Here are some extra stories and activities if you decide not to go on an all-day excursion:

Additional Stories, Activities, and Games:

- Have the children set a timer or watch the clock to see how long they can practice patience while waiting for something. For example, you could plan a game or activity that they can do if they can wait patiently for five minutes or another time frame that's appropriate for their age.
- Make a clock using paper or paper plates and crayons or markers.
- Another Bible story: Noah – God was patient while Noah built the ark – 1 Peter 3:20.

Kindness

Introduction

This was our 6th annual Grandkids Camp, and this year we had 5 grandchildren aged 7, 6, 5, 4, and 3. We have another grandchild who would be ready to join us the next year but just missed the cutoff this time of turning 2 years old.

Each day followed the same format as in previous years, featuring Bible lessons, crafts, activities, and snacks that tie in with the lessons. We always begin by reviewing our Bible verse and explaining it, along with the camp rules. Thankfully, some of the kids already have many of the rules memorized from past years!

Memory Verse: Ephesians 4:32

"*Be kind to one another, tenderhearted, forgiving one another as God in Christ Jesus forgave you.*"

Prepare a Kindness Jar

Label a jar as "Kindness Jar" and place it where the children will see it regularly—like on the table where we eat and do crafts. Fill the jar with small treats, such as M&M's or Skittles. Encourage the kids to notice when someone does something kind so that person can receive a treat. They can also give a treat to someone who shows them kindness.

Of course, grandparents will be on the lookout for kind acts and will hand out treats as well. For younger children, you may need to establish a rule that they shouldn't announce their own kind deeds, only those they observe in siblings or cousins. At first, this can be quite challenging. One child even expressed frustration about not receiving recognition for his kindness and said, "I'm not going to say what kind things the others did anymore because they aren't noticing what I did that was kind." This turned into a valuable teaching moment. I reminded him that focusing on our actions of kindness rather than seeking praise is truly what kindness is about. Remember, our actions are seen by God, and that's what matters most!

Books to read at bedtime that you can purchase or get from the local library:

- *The Berenstain Bears and Too Much Teasing* by Stan and Jan Berenstain
- *Papa's Pastries* by Charles Toscano
- *Let's be Kind* by PK Hallinan

Kindness: Day One

Discussion Questions to Introduce the Theme:

1. Do you know what kindness is? Kindness can be expressed through our thoughts, actions, and words. It embodies being generous, considerate, and friendly. At its core, kindness involves helping others and showing compassion.
2. How many of you feel you are kind all the time? (Pause for responses.)

3. Is there anyone who is kind all the time? The truth is, none of us are kind all the time but God is. God showed His greatest kindness to us by extending us grace and forgiveness for our sin. He extends kindness and grace to wicked and ungrateful people. It can be especially easy to be unkind to our family and friends because we are all sinner
4. How can we learn more about kindness? (By reading God's Word and understanding His kindness and grace for us)

Review Bible Verse: Ephesians 4:32 – "*Be kind to one another, tenderhearted, forgiving one another as God in Christ Jesus forgave you.*"

What is this verse telling us about how to be kind?

Possible Songs:

These are both good songs to teach the children and help them learn the verse found on YouTube - Cops and Robbers "Be Kind and Compassionate [7]"

"Be Kind Everyday[8]"

I shared one song with our grandchildren, and they didn't care for it, so we didn't end up using it. They were, however, still singing the song from last year. They even sang it when I was not being very patient with them as a reminder to me.

Bible Story: Healing the Leper—Matthew 8:1-4

Discussion Questions Before Reading the Story:

1. What do you think leprosy is? Give them some time to share their thoughts—it could lead to some interesting answers!

---

[7] https://www.youtube.com/watch?v=-FceQml15sY
[8] https://www.youtube.com/watch?v=sazIIKrJbL8

Leprosy is caused by slowly growing bacteria and is quite rare in the U.S. today, but it still affects people in poorer countries where access to clean water, nutritious food, and sanitary living conditions is limited. It can look very ugly. The disease can manifest as a bumpy rash that may appear on the face, nose, eyes, or any other area of skin. If left untreated, it can spread and lead to the loss of fingers or toes.

2. Does that help you picture what leprosy might look like?
3. In Biblical times, many believed that leprosy was a punishment for sins or something bad that you did. Do you think that's true?
4. People with leprosy were required to live outside the city, often alone or with others who had the disease. Many people avoided lepers, fearing they could catch it. Lepers even had to shout "unclean" to warn others not to come close. How would that make you feel?

Read Matthew 8:1-4

Discussion Questions:

1. What did Jesus do that most people wouldn't? He touched the man with leprosy.
2. What do you think those who witnessed it thought? Perhaps they feared he would catch the disease too.
3. What did Jesus tell the man to do? He asked him not to tell anyone and to go to the priest.
4. Why? Visiting the priest would determine if he was truly healed, allowing him to return to the city.
5. Did the man follow Jesus's instructions? No, he spread the word about what happened.
6. If you were healed from a serious illness, wouldn't you want to share the news? It would be hard to keep it a secret, right?
7. Do you think Jesus showed kindness? Absolutely! Regardless of how you look or what you've done, Jesus loves you and extends

kindness to everyone. He demonstrated the ultimate kindness by dying on the cross for our sins.

All of us who have been "healed" from our sin by accepting the forgiveness of Jesus have experienced what the leper experienced. He could not heal himself and was destined to die, and we cannot get rid of our sin ourselves and are destined to an eternal death (separation from God), unless we let Jesus cleanse us from our sin. This should cause us to share the good news with others too.

Reflection:

The day after this lesson, one of the grandchildren had an allergic reaction and developed a rash on his back. A cousin even asked if it was leprosy! At least they were paying attention!

Object Lesson: Rotten banana or ripe banana

Supplies:

- Rotten banana
- Ripe banana

Begin by holding up a rotten banana and ask the children, "Would you want to eat this?" When they answer "no," agree with them and explain, "I wouldn't want to either." Then ask, "Why not?" Point out that it's brown, mushy, and looks like something we'd throw away.

Next, hold up a ripe banana and ask, "Who would want to eat this one?" Most children will likely say yes—it's yellow, ripe, and looks tasty.

Now say:

Did you know our lives can be like these two bananas? The rotten banana represents people who act unkindly and make bad choices. The ripe banana represents those who are kind and make good choices. Which kind of banana do you think God wants us to be like?

(Wait for responses.)

"That's right—the ripe banana!"

Connect it to the story:

In our story, who was like the ripe banana? Jesus—our perfect example. We should live like Him. Was there anyone in the story who acted like the rotten banana? Yes, the people who didn't want to be around the leper.

Wrap up with reflection questions:

When we show kindness to others, which banana are we being like? And when we say hurtful things, hit, or take something away from someone, which banana do we act like?

Snack: Bananas

After the discussion, let the children taste the ripe bananas. You can share one banana among them or provide enough for each child to have their own. To make it extra special, consider offering peanut butter or chocolate for dipping. Some might choose peanut butter, while others may prefer chocolate. None of our grandchildren had a banana with either of these options before.

Crafts: Soap Carving

Supplies:

- One bar of Ivory soap for each child (Ivory soap is affordable and easy to work with.)
- A plastic knife for each child
- Small cookie cutters

Instructions:

1. Unwrap the soap. Then either you or one of the children can gently rub off the "Ivory" label from the surface.

2. To make a carving, press a cookie cutter firmly into the soap. If it doesn't cut all the way through, use a plastic knife to carefully trim around the edges.
3. You can encourage the children to get creative—some may want to make their own designs, while others might prefer using the cookie cutters as a guide.

When we did this activity, we found that the soap was a little too soft and sometimes crumbled. Still, it worked well when we used cookie cutters that went all the way through, rather than trying to carve freehand. The kids really enjoyed experimenting and tried their best to make something unique.

At the end, we saved a few bars of soap for handwashing in the bathroom, and we bagged up the rest with each child's name so they could take them home and show their parents.

As a final reminder during the activity, we told the children that while the soap is fun to use, it can't wash away leprosy—only Jesus could do that. And just like with sin, we can't clean ourselves with soap or by doing good things. Only Jesus can wash away our sins through His sacrifice on the cross.

Activity: First-Aid Kit

If you have a first-aid kit, show the contents to the children. We encouraged each child to create their own first-aid kit, so they were prepared to show kindness toward anyone who might get hurt during the week.

Supplies:

- 3-5 Band-Aids per child
- One sheet of white cardstock per child
- Red paper or marker

- Black cardstock for cutting out handles
- Cotton balls
- Q-tips
- Tape

Instructions:

1. Fold your white cardstock in half. Cut a 1-inch strip from the black paper and glue or tape one end to each edge opposite the fold—these will be your handles for easy carrying.
2. Then, cut red paper into strips and glue them on as a plus sign, one on each side of the folded cardstock. If you prefer, you can simply draw the plus signs with a red marker instead.
3. Next, use extra paper to create little pockets inside your kit. These are great for holding Band-Aids, cotton balls, Q-tips, or any other small first-aid items. Feel free to include anything age-appropriate. We added several Band-Aids, cotton balls, pre-packaged alcohol wipes, and Q-tips to ours.

You'll find that kids love using Band-Aids! When we did this activity, they even used their kits to help PaQ when he accidentally burned himself with a glue gun later. We also had one grandchild who collected all the Band-Aids from the other kits, but we made sure the grandchild returned them!

Activity: Outdoor walk

Discussion Questions:

1. Did you know that to Jesus, it doesn't matter what you've done, how you look, or what others think of you or say about you? Jesus created you and loves you unconditionally. He is always reaching out to show us just how much He loves and cares.
2. What are some ways you think Jesus expresses His love for us every day through the beautiful things around us?

3. Does He show His love through the creation of flowers and trees? Through animals? Or maybe through the love of our grandparents and parents? God's love is everywhere!

Take a walk and pay attention to the beautiful things outside—these are God's ways of showing His love and kindness through creation. Feel free to collect lovely items, especially pinecones for tomorrow's craft. Ask the kids to make a list of all the beautiful things they observe outdoors.

Craft: Collage

Create a collage of all the beautiful things you observed by using pictures from magazines. We also let the children glue the items they collected onto sturdy paper plates. It's wonderful to see what each child considers beautiful! One child's plate might be filled with rocks, while others showcase ferns, moss, mushrooms, acorns, and pinecones. Truly, all of God's creation is beautiful!

Craft: Butterfly

Supplies:

- Several colors of tissue paper
- Sandwich zip-lock bags
- Pipe cleaners

Instructions:

1. Tear pieces of different colored tissue paper and place them into the zip-lock bags, being careful not to overfill them.
2. Scrunch the zip-lock bag from the middle and secure it with a pipe cleaner, shaping the bag so that each side resembles butterfly wings.
3. Use another pipe cleaner to create antennae for your butterfly.

One of our grandchildren is really into butterflies this year, so we decided to do this fun and simple craft! It's perfect for children of all ages.

Craft: Flower

Here's a fun way to create a beautiful flower using a paper plate:

Supplies:

- Paper plates
- Paint, markers, or crayons
- Scissors
- Paint stirrers
- Green and/or brown construction paper
- Glue or tape

Instructions:

1. Have the children color or paint the entire plate.
2. Cut petals from the outer edge of the plate toward the center, leaving the circle in the middle as the flower's center.
3. For the stem, use paint stir sticks or cut a stem and attach leaves cut from green construction paper.
4. Let the children color the stick/stem green or brown.

This craft allows for lots of creativity and results in lovely flowers!

Activity: The Kindness Game[9]

Gather the children in a circle and have a ball or beanbag ready. Begin by having a grandparent demonstrate how the game works: Gently toss the ball to each child one at a time, and with each toss, share something kind about that child. This could be a compliment about their personality, a thoughtful action they've taken, or a way they've shown kindness to others.

---

[9] Adapted from "12 Simple Preschool Kindness Activities – Play the Kindness Game," by Tanja McIlroy, 2025, Empowered Parents, (https://empoweredparents.co/preschool-kindness-activities/). Adapted with permission. Permission granted by author on March 3, 2025.

Once the demonstration is complete, invite the children to play. They'll take turns tossing the ball or beanbag to someone in the circle, making sure each person gets a turn. When they pass the ball, they should say something kind about the person they're giving it to.

We found that younger children often struggle to come up with kind things to say, so we provided them with some suggestions to help.

Kindness: Day Two

Bible Story: Ruth 1-4—Ruth & Naomi

If the children are old enough and are able to sit still, read the entire book of Ruth from *The Message Bible*. For younger children or those with shorter attention spans, *The Beginners Bible* offers a concise version. You can also paraphrase the story, emphasizing the theme of kindness throughout.

Discussion Questions:

1. Who showed kindness in the story?
2. How did they demonstrate it? Ruth stayed with Naomi and went to a foreign country. Boaz showed grace and kindness to Ruth by allowing her to glean in his fields, giving her water and food.
3. Was Ruth a good friend to Naomi?
4. In what ways did Boaz show kindness to Ruth?
5. How does Boaz's marriage and redeeming of Ruth reflect what Jesus did for us? Boaz was her kinsman-redeemer, buying back Ruth and Naomi's land and marrying Ruth. This is just like Jesus redeeming humanity from sin and death.

Finally, encourage them to think about how they can show kindness to others in similar ways as Ruth and Boaz.

Craft: Ruth Showed Kindness by Going with Naomi— "Where You Go, I Will Go"

Supplies:

- Cardstock for each child's feet
- One straw per child, cut in half (I bought straws that were big enough for a pencil to fit inside.)
- Two sticks (like pencils or rounded sticks) for each child—they need to fit inside the straws, and they should be about the same length.
- One duct tape tube per child. We purchased one duct tape roll per child in different colors for easy identification (purchase at a dollar store).

Instructions:

1. Use cardstock to trace the children's feet and cut them out.
2. On the left foot, write "Where you go, I will go," and on the right foot, write "Where you stay, I will stay." Or you can simplify as we did in the picture on the following page.
3. Tape the cut straws to the inside bottom of each foot, just below the big toe.
4. Tape the sticks inside the duct tape tube on opposite sides, positioning one stick at the top and the other at the bottom of the tube.
5. Slide the straws over the sticks. When the children roll the tube, it will look like their feet are walking.

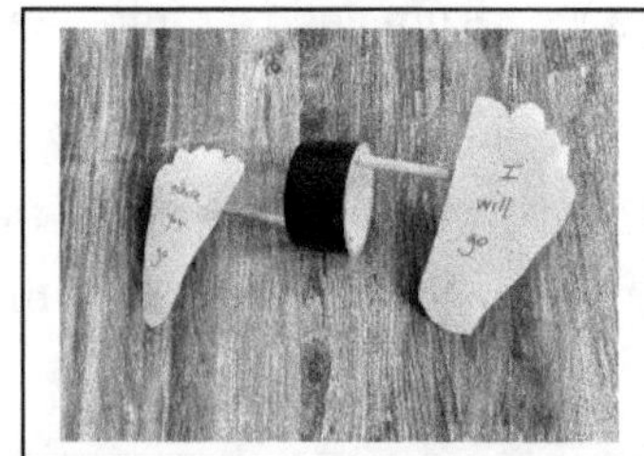

To ensure the feet go straight, make sure the sticks are of equal length and positioned correctly. They should not only be on opposite sides of the inside of the tape tube but also one on the top and one on the bottom. Enjoy creating and discussing how Ruth's kindness reflects in this fun activity! The children will enjoy rolling (walking) their feet across the floor, so clear plenty of space.

Craft: Paper Plate Baskets for Gleaning Wheat[10]

Supplies:

- One paper plate for each child
- 18 inches of ribbon for each child
- Stickers
- Crayons
- 4-5 grains for each child (available at craft stores like Michaels, used as decorations in flower arrangements)

Prepare the Area: Before starting, hide the grains around the designated area where the children will "glean" later.

Instructions:

1. Fold the entire plate in half.
2. Attach the ribbon to the top opening of the plate to create a handle by stapling or taping it in place on both sides of the opening.
3. Allow the children to decorate their baskets using crayons and stickers.

Activity: Scavenger Hunt for Grain

Once the baskets are completed, send the children on a scavenger hunt around the house to find the hidden grains, just like Ruth collected grain for Naomi and put it in her basket. Let them know they should gather their allotted number of grains (about five for each child) and return to the table when they're finished.

---

[10] Adapted from "Ruth Kid's Lesson" by Carrie Butler, 2019, Stretching Cents. Adapted with permission. Permission granted by author on March 6, 2025.

To make it easier for the baskets, consider cutting the grain stems shorter, as the long ones can be a bit unwieldy. This will help the grains fit nicely into their baskets. Enjoy the hunt!

Snack: Chex Mix

Start by asking the children what they think is made from grain or wheat. Encourage them to come up with as many items as they can. Let them know that cereal is one example.

You can either make Chex Mix together or purchase it premade. If you choose to make it, you can use the classic recipe found on the Chex cereal box. For convenience, I ended up buying a couple of bags, but as the children get older, they might enjoy making it together! Enjoy the tasty treat!

Craft: Flip flop wreath

Supplies:

- Wreath form (flat), wreath cut from cardboard or a large circle cut from cardboard–one per child (Warning: a metal wreath form does not work well for this craft.)
- 4-6 pairs of flip flops per child
- Ribbon to decorate and hang
- Hot glue gun & extra glue sticks
- Embellishments to decorate, such as silk flowers, sunglasses, letters to spell kindness, or a sign to add to the bottom or top that has the verse or "where you go, I will go." Let the children choose.

Instructions:

1. Lay out the flip flops in the pattern they desire.
2. Put glue on the same place on each flip flop, either right below or above the two holds of the strap.

3. Continue all around the wreath form and leave a spot at the bottom for flowers, ribbon, or a small sign that says "Kindness."
4. Add a ribbon to hang.
5. If you have different embellishments, let them decorate as they wish.

Kindness: Day Three

Bible Story: John 4:4-14 (*The Message Bible*)—The Woman at the Well

Discussion questions:

1. Why do you think Jews didn't associate with Samaritans? The Samaritan woman was seen as a foreigner and a Gentile, which meant Jews typically wouldn't interact with her. In fact, speaking to a Gentile was often frowned upon.
2. Is that a kind way to treat someone?
3. Do you see this happening today? Can you think of any examples?
4. Did Jesus care that she was a Samaritan? No, He wanted to share His good news with everyone.
5. What was the good news that Jesus shared?
6. Should we only be kind to people who look like us, act like us, believe like us, or attend our church? No! God calls us to be kind to everyone.

Jesus broke through the prejudices that others held, reminding us that kindness and the gift of salvation should be extended to all, regardless of race, skin color, or religious beliefs. We should strive to be kind to everyone!

Gospel Opportunity

Use this idea or share from your own heart that Jesus shows the greatest act of kindness when He forgives us:

"When we are struggling to be kind to another person, we should remember God's great kindness toward us. As sinners, we have offended God. The Bible says that we have even hated Him. So, God had every right to be angry with us, but instead He showed just how great His kindness is by saving us! When you really want to respond to someone with unkindness, think of how God could have punished you for your sin. But instead, in His kindness, He offers everyone here complete forgiveness! Every day we still sin against God, and He continues to be kind to us. Let's show the kindness to others that God has shown to us! This is possible only if we abide in Him, by getting to know Him more and more through praying, reading and learning His Word, and following Him." [11]

Activity: Sponsor a Compassion Child

This is a wonderful opportunity for older children, who are earning money or receiving an allowance, to learn about kindness and generosity by sponsoring a child through Compassion International. Encourage your grandkids to participate by writing letters and contributing some of their own money for sponsorship. It's a good idea to discuss this with their parents before Grandkids Camp, so everyone is on board with the kids using their resources. Alternatively, you could sponsor a child on their behalf.

You can either choose a child in advance and prepare everything for the kids to meet and write letters during camp or let the children select the

---

[11] Adapted From "Kindness Bible Lesson (Fruit of the Spirt)," by Kara Jenkins, Ministry-to-Children by Tony Kumer, (https://ministry-to-children.com/kindness-bible-lesson-fruit-of-the-spirit/) - Copyright © 2025 **Creative Commons Attribution-ShareAlike 4.0 International**.

child they want to sponsor together. If you decide to go this route, make sure to involve them in the monthly support and the letter-writing process.

When our children were younger, we sponsored a couple of children through Compassion International and even had the chance to visit them in the Philippines. It was an incredible experience, and we still keep in touch through social media with the two sisters we sponsored.

Activity: Toothpaste Experiment

We did this fun activity with our children when they were in elementary and middle school to encourage them to speak kindly to one another.

Supplies:

- Small or full-size tube of toothpaste for each child or team
- Paper plates
- Plastic spoons

Instructions:

Start by giving each child or team a tube of toothpaste, a paper plate, and a plastic spoon. Ask them to squeeze the entire tube of toothpaste onto their plates as quickly as they can, making it a friendly competition. They'll enjoy this part and will likely have a blast. You may even set a timer to make it a contest. One of our grandkids squeezed so hard that her tube burst at the other end, leaving her with toothpaste all over her hands!

Next, present them with the challenge of getting all the toothpaste back into the tube. Offer them a spoon and promise a reward if they can manage it. Let them try until they give up and then use this as a teaching moment. We gave them a few minutes, and their comments during the attempt were priceless. One child focused intently without saying a word, while others exclaimed, "That's too much," "I don't think we can do this," "What a mess!" and "This is impossible." "How much time do we have?" "Ugh, it's covering the top, I won't be able to get the lid on."

These reactions made it easy to discuss how unkind and mean words are like toothpaste. Once spoken, they can't be taken back, no matter how hard we try.

Side Note: When my kids did this, they were so competitive that they even tried putting the toothpaste in their mouths and blowing it back into the tube—Spoiler alert: it didn't work!

Craft/Activity: Living Water Drops

Supplies:

- 9 oz. party cups
- Crayons or colored paper
- Scissors
- Stickers
- Blue cardstock

Instructions:

1. Before camp, draw water drop shapes on the blue card stock, small enough to fit inside the cups. Have the children (if old enough) cut out the water drop shapes. Make enough for each child to feature one word of the verse. For example, you could create four drops with the phrase "Be Kind to One Another," placing one or two words on one drop.
2. Let the older children create more drops for more of the verse.
3. Cover the cups with white paper for decorating or let the kids personalize clear cups directly with stickers and other decorations.
4. Have the children put the drops into their cups, then have them pour them out and put them in the correct order for the verse.
5. If the children are all old enough to read, you could make it a race to see who can complete it first.

Craft: Kindness to Wildlife—Creating a Bird Feeder

Supplies:

- Pinecones (collected during a walk)
- Peanut butter
- Small bowls or plates
- Birdseed
- Plastic knife
- String or twine (cut into 8-10 inch strips)
- Scissors

Instructions:

1. Start by scooping peanut butter into small bowls or plates, providing one for each child to streamline the process.
2. Place birdseed in additional bowls or plates, ensuring each child has their own. Set up a paper plate or tray for each child to work on, to keep things tidy. Consider doing this activity outdoors.
3. Each child should place their pinecone on the paper plate and thoroughly spread peanut butter over it, covering as much surface area as possible.
4. Next, the children can either sprinkle birdseed over the peanut butter-covered pinecone or roll it in the seeds on another plate—whichever they prefer.
5. After that, they can tie a piece of twine or string around the top of the pinecone. Hang the finished feeders in a tree outside so they can enjoy watching the birds during their time at camp. If they wish to take their feeders home, store them in a zip-lock bag to prevent a mess with the birdseed.

The children will have the joy of observing birds come to feed!

Kindness: Day Four

Bible Story: Luke 8:40-48 (*The Message Bible*)—Jesus Heals a Woman Who Touched His Clothes

Discussion Questions:

1. What was the first thing that Jesus did that was kind? He was on his way to Jarius's house to heal his daughter.
2. Were there a lot of people around Jesus?
3. How many years was the woman sick? Twelve years, longer than many of you have been alive.
4. What did the woman think she could do to get healed? She believed that if she could just touch the hem of His clothes, she would be healed.
5. How did Jesus know that someone touched Him when there was such a crowd around Him pushing and bumping? Even in the midst of the bustling crowd, Jesus sensed that someone had touched Him because He felt power go out from Him.
6. Why do you think the woman was trembling and didn't want to admit that she had touched Jesus at first? The woman was trembling and hesitant to admit that it was she who had touched Him because she felt she had secretly taken a miracle. She likely feared how Jesus would react.
7. Did Jesus reprimand her? No, Jesus did not reprimand her. He responded with kindness, compassion, and affirmation of her faith. He acknowledged her faith and reassured her, emphasizing His compassion and the importance of her healing. This interaction highlights the loving nature of Jesus and His willingness to help those in need. When we have faith in Jesus, He heals us from our sin. Anyone can experience God's power and grace if they have faith and believe in Jesus. It is not by works, social status, or outward appearance: God accepts us through faith.

Activity: "Who Touched Me?" Game

Setup: Have the children sit in a circle on the floor. One child will sit in the middle with a blindfold on.

Instructions:

1. Quietly point to one child in the circle to gently touch the child in the middle.
2. The child in the middle will try to guess who touched them. If they can't guess, switch to another child in the middle.
3. Continue rotating until each child has a turn.

Discussion:

After the game, talk with the children about how challenging it is to know who touched you when you can't see them. Ask them if they felt any "power" go out of them when they were touched. Remind them that, unlike Jesus, they can't sense others in that special way.

Activity: Touch Bag Game

Supplies:

- A small soft sack (like a string backpack)
- Familiar items (e.g. a pencil, toy car, coin, piece of fruit, spoon)

Instructions:

1. Place several recognizable items inside the bag, ensuring there's at least one item for each child.
2. Have the children take turns reaching into the bag without pulling anything out.
3. Each child should feel an item and guess what it is based solely on touch.
4. After guessing, they can pull the item out to see if they were correct.
   a. If they guessed right, keep the item out.

   b. If they guessed wrong, put it back in the bag.
5. Continue the game until the children tire of it or have guessed all the items.

Discussion: As they play, encourage the children to describe what they feel and share their thought processes. This activity enhances their tactile senses while having fun!

Craft: The Touch of Kindness

Supplies:

- Different colors of cardstock paper
- Markers or crayons

Instructions:

1. Begin by tracing each child's hands onto the cardstock paper.
2. In the center of the traced hands, write "The Touch of Kindness."
3. Encourage the children to think of ways they can show kindness. Ask them to write their ideas on each of their fingers. Suggestions might include:

   Help others
   Give a hug
   Say nice things
   Be patient
   Clean up toys
   Encourage others
   Give a back rub
   Hold a hand
   Offer a gentle touch
   Spend time with family
   Give to others
   Listen to a friend
4. Try to let them come up with their own answers rather than providing too many. You can take turns sharing ideas to ensure

everyone gets a chance to speak, starting with the youngest child for simpler suggestions. Our grandchildren, being seven and under, had a hard time coming up with things so we had to offer plenty of suggestions.

5. Once they have filled in all ten fingers, staple or tape the two hands together, either back-to-back or at the wrists, allowing all the ideas to be visible at once.
6. You can choose to leave the hands on the original paper rather than cutting them out, especially if time is short.

This colorful display will serve as a wonderful reminder for the children to take home, showcasing their creative ideas for spreading kindness!

Snacks:

Let the children get creative with a hands-on snack! Here are a couple of fun options:

1. **Peanut Butter Crackers or English Muffin:**
    a. Provide various types of crackers or muffins, peanut butter, and toppings like sliced bananas, raisins, or chocolate chips.
    b. Let the kids spread peanut butter on their crackers and add their favorite toppings to create their own delicious snacks!
2. **Mini Pizzas:**
    a. Use mini muffins (or English muffins) as the base.
    b. Offer a variety of toppings, such as tomato sauce, cheese, pepperoni, veggies, and herbs.
    c. Allow the children to assemble their own mini pizzas with the toppings they like best before baking them for a few minutes to melt the cheese.

Both options encourage creativity and give the children a chance to enjoy their creations!

Craft: Kindness Pet Rocks

Supplies:

- Smooth stones (gathered or chosen by the children)
- Acrylic paints or washable paint
- Paintbrushes
- Cups for water (for cleaning brushes)
- Paper towels (for drying brushes)
- Dark permanent markers (for writing)

Instructions:

1. **Gather Stones:** Have the children collect or choose fairly large, smooth stones that are suitable for painting.
2. **Paint the Rocks:** Provide paint and brushes and let the children paint their stones with vibrant colors. Encourage them to be creative!
3. **Brainstorm Kindness Words:** While the paint dries, gather the children and brainstorm words or phrases related to kindness. Examples might include:

   Love
   Share
   Smile
   Help
   Be kind
   You matter
   Spread joy
4. **Writing on the Rocks:** Once the paint is dry, let the children choose their favorite words or phrases. Grandparents or adults can write these on the rocks using dark permanent markers.
5. **Gift the Kindness Rocks:** Encourage the children to give their kindness rocks to someone special to brighten their day—friends, family, or even neighbors.

This activity blends creativity with a heartfelt message, enabling the children to spread kindness in a personal way by gifting their painted rocks to someone they want to uplift.

Goodness

Introduction

This year brought another wave of fun and excitement, with children aged 2 to 8 participating. It's hard to believe that when we first started, the oldest was just 2 years old! Our lessons are designed to suit both the 2-year-olds through 8-year-olds and beyond. We focused on meeting the individual needs of the kids in attendance.

We paired older children with younger ones, allowing the older kids to assist with tasks ranging from crafts to filling water bottles and ensuring everyone stays within set boundaries. The older children were eager to help the 2-year-olds, and aside from the littlest one, most have become quite independent and require minimal assistance.

Memory Verse: Galatians 6:9 (add verse 10 for older children).

"And let us not grow weary of doing good, for in due season we will reap, if we do not give up. So then as we have opportunity, let us do good to everyone."

The song this year was "Good Good Father" by Chris Tomlin. I played it for them on my phone throughout the day and during certain activities. By the end, they did pretty well at singing the chorus.

I also purchased the book God Thinks You Are Wonderful by Max Lucado, and I read it to them at least two times and let the children who could read, read it again to themselves.

See invitation appendix for this year's sample invitation. I informed the parents that our goodness theme included a donation of canned goods to a local food pantry, which is easy to find in any community. The pantry we identified specifically requested mac and cheese, so I let parents know they could opt to provide that instead of canned items. For older children who had their own money, I suggested that they select and purchase the canned goods to donate themselves.

On the final day, our last activity of the week was to drop off the bags of food on the way home. PaQ took all the children to the food pantry, where the oldest grandchild carried the bags to the door. Although the pantry was closed, we had arranged to leave the bags at the entrance.

Goodness: Day One

Define goodness for the children by helping them understand that goodness is about being kind and doing the right thing. Teach them that it means being virtuous and making choices that show care for others. When you take actions that reflect righteousness and treat people with respect and compassion, you are practicing goodness.

Explain that goodness is tied to the nature of God—He is the standard for all that is good. The gospel is the good news that God, in His goodness, offers salvation through Jesus and provides a way for you to have a relationship with Him.

Use this lesson to really teach what goodness means:[12]

Activity - Kindle Curiosity

Description: Build with canned goods to discover this week's theme of goodness

Supplies:

- 15-20 canned goods (8 of them will spell out "Goodness," one letter per can)
- Letters to add to the cans that spell out Goodness. I used Post-it notes.

Instructions:

1. Create a pyramid with the canned goods.
2. Challenge the children to find all the letters that spell the theme word without giving them hints.
3. Once they spell out "Goodness," read the verse for the week.

Discussion:

1. What is goodness?
2. How is it different from kindness? (Allow time for their responses.)
3. Explain that in this verse, goodness means not only being good but also doing good and encouraging others to do the same.
4. What are some good things we can do?

Reflection:

These cans of food represent a way for us to do good. In our community, many people struggle to afford food, and you can help make a difference.

---

[12] Adapted From "Goodness Bible Lesson (Fruit of the Spirt)," by Kara Jenkins, Ministry-to-Children by Tony Kumer, (https://ministry-to-children.com/goodness-bible-lesson-fruit-of-the-spirit/) - Copyright © 2025 **Creative Commons Attribution-ShareAlike 4.0 International**.

One simple way you can help is by donating food to those in need. Churches and schools often hold food drives, where you can bring canned or boxed food to share with others. There are also food pantries where people can go to get food for free—your donations help make that possible.

- Can you think of other ways we can do good for people in our community or around the world? (Examples: sharing the love of Jesus and the gospel message, picking up trash, clothing drives, buying gifts for children at Christmas, volunteering at homeless shelters, etc.)

Goodness is reflected not just in our actions, but also in the purity of our hearts. We are called to demonstrate the goodness of Christ in our daily lives. As Psalm 23:6 says, *"Surely goodness and mercy shall follow me all the days of my life, and I shall dwell in the house of the Lord forever."* This verse reminds us that goodness and mercy are constant companions, guiding us.

Memory Verse: Galatians 6:9-10a – "*And let us not grow weary of doing good, for in due season we will reap, if we do not give up. So then, as we have opportunity, let us do good to everyone*."

Bible story: 2 Chronicles 29:1-36—King Hezekiah

Read the passage from *The Message Bible* or summarize the story.

King Hezekiah stands out as one of the few righteous kings in a long line of mostly wicked rulers in Israel, Judah, and Jerusalem. He loved God and showed God's goodness through his actions and the decrees he made for Jerusalem and Judah.

Discussion Questions:

1. What did King Hezekiah do that showed goodness? One of his first acts was to reopen and repair the temple of the Lord, which

had fallen into disrepair and was neglected. He not only restored the temple physically, but also spiritually, commanding the people to turn away from idolatry and return to worshiping the one true God. Second Chronicles 29:2 notes that Hezekiah *"did what was right in the eyes of the Lord, according to all that David his father had done,"* emphasizing that Hezekiah was committed to the Lord to do what was right and good. His commitment to God was further demonstrated by his declaration in verse 10, where he says, *"Now it is in my heart to make a covenant with the LORD, the God of Israel."*

2. Why did King Hezekiah show goodness and lead the people to worship God again? Hezekiah's desire to lead the people back into a right relationship with God was fueled by his genuine love for the Lord and his dedication to upholding God's covenant. His actions showed that his heart was full of goodness because he sought to honor God above all else, desiring to lead Judah in faithfulness and obedience to God's will.

We too should help to lead others to worship God and have a right relationship with Him.

Craft/Activity: Cleansing the Temple

When we learn about the story of King Hezekiah, one of the first things we see him do as king is cleanse the temple. Can you imagine what he was getting rid of? All the bad stuff—like idols—and it was probably dirty from not being used for so long.

As you guide the children through this craft and activity, help them understand the importance of cleaning and making things holy, just like King Hezekiah did. We want them to see how honoring God sometimes starts with clearing out what doesn't belong.

Supplies:

- **Broom straw** – Can be ordered online or found at craft stores.
- **Short sticks or dowels** – You can buy these at hardware stores or gather sturdy sticks from outside. Each stick should be about the height of the child, so they can hold it comfortably.
- **Twine, rope, or wire** – To tie the broom straw onto the stick.
- **Floral wire or hot glue (optional)** – For extra support in holding the straw securely to the stick.

Instructions:

1. **Prepare the Materials:** Give each child a small bunch of broom straw. You can cut the straw into smaller pieces if needed. Provide each child with a stick (or dowel), making sure it is about the same length as them.
2. **Tie the Straw to the Stick:** Show the children how to gather the broom straw and attach it to their stick. Help them secure the straw with twine, rope, or wire. For extra security, you can use floral wire or a little hot glue to keep the straw from falling out. You may need to help them re-tie their brooms if the straw doesn't stay in place at first.
3. **Cleansing the Temple (Pretend Play):** Once the brooms are ready, encourage the children to "clean" a specific area of your house, porch, or even a play area. Set up a small space (such as a corner) and scatter some toys or even a little sand if you're feeling adventurous. The children can use their brooms to sweep away the "mess," imagining they are cleansing the temple of God, just like King Hezekiah did.

4. **Reflection and Takeaway:** After the activity, gather the children and explain that just like King Hezekiah cleansed the temple to make it holy and ready for worship, we should keep our

hearts clean for God. When they take their brooms home, remind them that the broom is a symbol to help them remember to keep their hearts pure, to worship God, and to show goodness to others.

This activity is not only fun but also a meaningful way for children to connect with the story of King Hezekiah and the importance of honoring God by keeping things holy and clean.

Activity: Joyous Worship

After the temple was cleaned, the people gathered to worship God. They sang, played instruments, bowed in reverence, and likely even danced in celebration.

Supplies:

- String
- Bells
- Stapler
- Hole punch
- Empty oatmeal containers or coffee cans with lids
- Sturdy paper plates

Instructions:

1. **String Bells**: Cut a small piece of string (about 6 inches), tie a bell to it, and form a loop so it can be shaken while worshiping.
2. **Drum**: Let the children decorate an empty oatmeal container or coffee can, which they can then use as a drum.
3. **Tambourine**: Staple two paper plates together, facing inward. Punch holes around the edges and tie a bell to each hole. Show the children how to use the tambourine. Each child should make an instrument to play.

Once the children have finished their crafts, it's time to sing and worship with their instruments and voices. Encourage them to dance in praise as well!

Use a song of your choice but I love the song from Psalm 100 by Leona Von Brethorst: "I will enter His gate with thanksgiving in my heart." This is a perfect song to sing, dance, and play their instruments.

We also played "Good, Good Father" for the children to worship with their instruments.

Remind the children that when they take their instruments home, they can use them as a reminder to worship God with the joy and goodness He has placed in their hearts. Let their instruments be a tool to continue praising Him wherever they are.

Craft: Helping Hand

Show goodness by lending a helping hand.

Supplies:

- 6" diameter pie tin (available at the dollar store)
- 16" ribbon
- 1-pound package of patching plaster or Plaster of Paris
- Gold spray paint
- Vaseline
- Baby oil or cooking spray (for the tin and the children's hands)
- Plastic stick (to write their name)
- Wet paper towels
- Newspaper
- Disposable bowl

Instructions:

1. **Prepare the Pie Tin:** Begin by coating the inside of the pie tin with a light film of Vaseline, baby oil, or cooking spray. This will help prevent the plaster from sticking.

2. **Mix the Plaster:** In a disposable bowl, mix the patching plaster with water, following the instructions on the package. Stir until you have a thick, smooth consistency. You'll need to work quickly, so mix one batch of plaster for each handprint. The first one took longer to get hard, but after that, they seemed to harden quickly.
3. **Prepare for Handprint:** Place a loop of ribbon in the pie tin, ensuring the loop extends outside the plate (this step is optional but can be used to hang the finished handprint). Pour the mixed plaster into the tin until it's about half-full.
4. **Make the Handprint:** Spray the child's hand lightly with cooking spray to prevent the plaster from sticking. Before the plaster sets, have the child press their hand firmly into the center of the mixture. Hold the hand in place for a few seconds to a couple of minutes, depending on the consistency of the plaster. For ours, we simply pressed the hand in, then quickly removed it. You will need two adults to help with this. One to mix and one to help the children place their hands in the plaster at the right time.
5. **Add the Child's Name:** Before the plaster hardens too much, use a plastic stick or similar tool to write the child's name (or initials) and the date underneath the handprint.
6. **Drying:** Let the plaster dry overnight.
7. **Painting:** Once dry, spray-paint both sides of the handprint with gold or silver spray paint for a beautiful finish.
8. **Gift to Parents:** The finished handprint can be given to the children's parents as a special reminder of their commitment to show goodness by lending a helping hand.

This craft not only creates a lasting keepsake but also teaches the children the value of helping others with a kind heart.

Goodness: Day Two

Bible Story: Mark 14 and John 13-14—Jesus Washing the Disciples' Feet

Read the Scripture or the "The Servant King" story from *The Jesus Storybook Bible.*

Warm-up Questions:

1. What kinds of things make your feet dirty or smelly? Does anyone have smelly feet right now?
2. Would you want to wash someone else's feet if they were really dirty or stinky?
3. What's the dirtiest job or chore you've ever had to do? What's the dirtiest job you can imagine?

Begin reading the story, but pause to ask: Would you want to wash someone's stinky feet? Who do you think should do it?

Discussion Questions:

1. Was what Jesus did—washing the disciples' feet—an act of goodness? Yes, despite Him being their Lord and Teacher, He became a servant and washed their feet. This showed His goodness and humility.
2. What was Jesus's greatest act of goodness? Jesus washed the disciples' feet, which made them clean, and His death and resurrection offers us cleansing from our sin and forgiveness.
3. Jesus said, "Do this for each other." What do you think He meant by that? Should we wash each other's feet today? We should serve others with humility and love, which represents the goodness of God.
4. How can we "do this for each other"? By doing good things for others, serving them, and telling them about Jesus. Jesus was teaching His disciples that the most important thing is to put the

needs of others above our own. And this applies to us too. God showed us His love and goodness by sending Jesus, and Jesus showed His love and goodness by serving us. He wants us to follow His example and put others first by serving them.

Craft: Make Bath Salts Gifts[13]

Supplies:

- Pickling salt (or any coarse salt)
- Epsom salt
- Food coloring
- Essential oils
- Baby food jars or small jars
- Bowls for mixing
- Spoons
- Ribbon
- Labels with the verse of the week

Instructions:

1. In a bowl, combine the pickling salt and Epsom salt equal amounts of each depending on how many jars you are filling.
2. Add a few drops of food coloring to the salt mixture. (Go light on the coloring—pastel shades work best.)
3. Add several drops of your chosen essential oil. Lavender is perfect for relaxation, while peppermint is invigorating. Mix thoroughly.
4. Carefully scoop the scented salt into baby food jars or other small jars.

---

[13] Adapted from "Jesus Washes the Disciples' Feet", by Jonathan and Michelle Minter,
© Teach Us the Bible, 2025
(https://www.teachusthebible.com/Lesson.php?Lesson=jesus-washes-the-disciples-feet). Adapted with permission. Permission granted by author on March 5, 2025.

5. Tie a decorative ribbon around the jar for a lovely touch.
6. Attach a label to each jar with a Bible verse or the verse of the week, so the recipient is reminded of the Scripture as they enjoy their bath.
7. Give the jar of bath salts as a thoughtful, personalized gift to someone.

Activity: Soapy Bubbles[14]

Recommended to do outdoors

Bubbles are made from soap, which is great for cleaning!

Supplies:

- Bubbles (You can use the bubble recipe from page 36 or the recipe section to make your own.)
- Bare feet
- Chairs

Instructions:

1. Arrange the chairs in a row for a small group of children or have them sit on the ground.
2. Blow bubbles and encourage the children to pop them using their toes.
3. After the activity, you can follow up by washing their feet for an extra fun and clean experience!

---

[14] Adapted from "Jesus Washes the Disciples' Feet", by Jonathan and Michelle Minter,
© Teach Us the Bible, 2025
(https://www.teachusthebible.com/Lesson.php?Lesson=jesus-washes-the-disciples-feet). Adapted with permission. Permission granted by author on March 5, 2025.

Craft: That's Yucky

Supplies:

- Paper
- Markers

Instructions:

1. Ask the children to think of foods they consider "yucky" or foods that make a big mess. Examples could include spilled salsa, chili with beans, old guacamole, or moldy cheese.
2. Give each child a piece of paper and some markers.
3. Encourage them to draw a picture of the messiest, grossest food they can imagine cleaning up. They can even combine different foods to create a really messy combination!
4. Once everyone has finished their drawings, hold up each picture one by one. Ask the other children to guess what it is.
5. If no one can guess, the artist can explain what it is and why they wouldn't want to clean it up. You can agree and say, "I DEFINITELY wouldn't want to eat or clean that!"
6. Wrap up by connecting the activity to the lesson: "Today we learned about a man who took care of the messiest job at a meal, even though He was the most important person there. Do you think you could show kindness and goodness like Jesus did?"

Activity: Slapjack Game

Supplies:

- A Deck of Cards

Instructions:

1. Gather the children together and have them sit in a circle on the floor. If you have more than eight grandkids, divide them into two groups and give each group a deck of cards.

2. Deal all the cards evenly among the players.

How to Play:

1. Players take turns going around the circle, placing one card face up in the middle.
2. When a Jack (or Joker, if you prefer) is placed in the middle, everyone tries to slap their hand down first. Make sure to show younger children what the Jack looks like so they can recognize it.
3. The first player to slap the Jack, or the player whose hand lands on the bottom of the pile, wins all the cards in the pile.
4. The winner places those cards at the bottom of their deck, and the game continues.
5. If a player runs out of cards, they are out of the game.
6. The game ends when one player has collected all the cards or when time runs out. The player with the most cards at the end is the winner.

Reflection on Winning in Slapjack:

Usually, when we think about winning a game, we picture being "on top"—being the first to finish or getting rid of all our cards. But in the game of Slapjack, the goal is to get to the bottom of the pile of hands faster than anyone else! Being at the bottom is often seen as a bad thing, but in this game, it's actually the key to winning.

This is a great opportunity to think about how the world views success versus how Jesus teaches us to live. In life, it's often tempting to want to be first or to be the one in charge. But Jesus shows us that true greatness comes from serving others and being willing to take the lowest position, just as He did when He washed His disciples' feet.

So, today, we can remember that, like in Slapjack, sometimes it's better to choose the "bottom" to serve and love others, instead of always striving to be "on top."

Goodness: Day Three

Bible Story: Queen Esther

Read "The Brave Queen" from *The Jesus Storybook Bible*, page 240.

Bible Truth: Goodness inspires righteous actions, even when it's difficult.

Discussion Questions:

1. How did Esther demonstrate goodness? Her actions delivered the Jewish people from death.
2. Did Haman show goodness?
3. Who else has delivered people from death? Jesus's sacrifice delivers those who believe from eternal death and separation from God.
4. Who received glory in the story of Esther? I'm sure the children will say Mordecai. But ultimately, it was God who deserved the glory, for it was His plan all along to deliver the Jews and reveal His great power and sovereignty. God used Esther and Mordecai as part of His divine purpose—and He can use you and me as well, when we choose to follow Him and bring glory to His name.

Crafts: King or Queen Crowns

Supplies:

- Poster board (purple, yellow, or any royal color)
- Pencil
- Scissors
- Glue
- Sequins
- Glitter
- Markers
- Stickers
- Tape or Stapler

Instructions:

1. **Prepare the crowns**: Before Grandkids Camp starts, draw and cut out enough crown shapes for each child. You can typically get four crowns from each poster board.
2. **Distribute and decorate**: Give each child a crown and let them decorate it using sequins, glitter, stickers, and markers—whatever they like to make it beautiful. Encourage creativity but remind them to leave some space near the ends so you can connect the ends once they are finished.
3. **Fit the crowns**: Once the children are done decorating, size the crowns to fit their heads. Use tape or staples to secure the ends together.
4. **Showtime**: Let the children model their crowns. They'll love posing for photos as little kings and queens!

Snack: Sharing homemade cookies to show goodness to others.

Supplies:

- Sugar cookie dough - purchase or make your own
- Whipped frosting
- Knife or spreader
- Plastic wrap
- Paper lunch bags

Instructions:

1. **Bake the Cookies:**
   Bake the cookies together. You can use a simple sugar cookie recipe or save time by purchasing premade sugar cookie dough from the store. This is a great option if you're working with younger children, as it's easier and quicker. Since we had 6 children, 8 years old and under, premade dough was the best

choice. Slice and bake the cookies according to the package instructions.

2. **Make Sandwich Cookies:**
   Once the cookies have cooled, have each child pick two cookies that are roughly the same size and shape. Show them how to spread frosting (store-bought whipped frosting works best for easy spreading) on the bottom of one cookie and then place the bottom of the other cookie on top to make a sandwich. This is a fun and simple way to create tasty treats! If needed, you can assist with the frosting or let the children do as much as they can on their own.
3. **Wrap and Decorate:**
   After they've made their sandwich cookies, demonstrate how to wrap them in plastic wrap (Saran wrap). This keeps the cookies fresh and makes them easy to gift. Next, have the children decorate a lunch bag or gift bag with markers, stickers, or other supplies. This adds a personal touch and helps them understand the importance of making their gift special.
4. **Show Goodness by giving the cookies away:**
   Explain to the children that sharing their cookies will help them practice goodness. Ask them to think about someone outside of camp who might enjoy receiving the cookies. Suggest giving them to a neighbor, a friend, or someone who might be in need. If they decide to share with a local neighbor, you can all go together to deliver the cookies. If they plan to give the cookies after camp, you can store them in the freezer until they're ready to take home.

Goal: The purpose of this activity is to teach the children how small acts of goodness—like sharing cookies—can bring joy to others. By thinking about someone else and offering a sweet treat, they learn the value of goodness, generosity, and the joy of giving.

Be sure to save some cookies for their snack time.

We ran out of time and energy to make the frosting and decorate the cookies, but we did manage to take a few over to one of our neighbors. This neighbor had given the kids some puzzles and other toys they had cleaned out of their house. I had the oldest write a thank-you note on the paper bag, and the rest of the children signed their names.

Craft: Bracelet Craft—Nature's Jewels

Introduction -Do you think kings and queens wore jewelry? Let's make our own bracelets while we go on a nature walk!

Supplies:

- Scissors
- Duct tape
- Treasures found on the walk

Start by cutting a piece of duct tape for each child, then wrap it around their wrist with the sticky side facing outward and the non-sticky side against their skin. As they walk, they can collect "jewels" or treasures from nature—like leaves, small flowers, or stones—and stick them to the sticky side of the tape, creating a unique bracelet.

Make sure to take some photos, as this might be a craft they can't take home with them. After they finish, we let the kids choose a spot to hang their bracelets around the house, garage, or outdoor areas. I ended up finding them in different places for days after they left, and it made me smile!

Goodness: Day Four

Bible Story: Genesis 1-2—The Story of Creation shows God's Goodness

Read "The Beginning" from *The Beginners Bible*, or "The Beginning: A Perfect Home." from the *Jesus Storybook Bible*.

We can see God's goodness not only in the way He loves, protects, and cares for us but also in the world around us—in creation. But what is creation? Creation is everything God made, and it reflects His nature, character, creativity, and goodness. The beauty and order of the world point us to the Creator Himself.

God is good and loving to us all the time. It is only through His power working in our hearts that He can produce goodness in our hearts.

Discussion Questions:

1. What do you think it might have been like to live in the Garden of Eden? It was perfect.
2. How do you think it might have felt to have God walk with you in the Garden of Eden? Adam and Eve were in perfect fellowship, and that is what God wanted.
3. What happened to the fellowship Adam and Eve had with God? Sin separated them from God.
4. Is there a way to restore that fellowship with God? God in His goodness sent Jesus to take the punishment we all deserve for our sin so we can have fellowship again with God.

Object Lesson: The Heart Inside

Supplies:

- 1 banana for each child
- Sharpie markers

Instructions:

1. **Pass out the bananas**: Give each child a banana to hold.

2. **Decorate the bananas**: Instruct the children to decorate the outside of their bananas using the Sharpie markers. They can draw designs, write words, or just have fun with their creativity.
3. **Peel the bananas**: Once everyone has finished decorating, ask them to peel their bananas.

   Talk about the lesson: As they peel back the banana skin, discuss how the outside of a person (or the outside of the banana) doesn't always show what's inside—what's in a person's heart. Only God sees the true condition of our hearts. The outside can be decorated, just like the banana's peel, but it's the inside that matters most. The Holy Spirit is the one who works in us, helping to create goodness and love in our hearts.
4. **Brown spots as a teaching moment**: If any of the bananas have brown spots, use that as an opportunity to talk about how we sometimes judge others based on their outward appearance. The brown spots remind us that what we see on the outside doesn't always reflect what's on the inside. Just like the banana's brown spots don't tell us how sweet or tasty the inside might be, we cannot judge if someone has goodness in their heart just by looking at them. Only God knows a person's heart.
5. **Important Note**: Be prepared for a bit of mess! The markers might not only end up on the banana peel only, but also on the children's hands. Don't worry—hands can be washed, and the mess is part of the fun! Enjoy the lesson, regardless of the cleanup.

This object lesson serves as a great reminder that we should focus on the inner qualities that only God can see, rather than judging others by their outward appearance.

Snack: Smoothies

Ingredients:

- 1 cup frozen blueberries or strawberries
- 1/2 cup vanilla (or plain) Greek yogurt

- 1 cup of your favorite milk
- 1 frozen banana (or use fresh ones from the lesson above if you still have them)
- Optional: honey, to taste

Instructions:

Place all the ingredients into the blender and blend until smooth. Pour, enjoy, and savor the deliciousness!

Craft: Citrus Stamps Craft

Supplies:

- Cardstock
- Lemons, limes, oranges, and/or grapefruit
- Paint (various colors)
- Plate(s) for paint
- Knife (to cut fruit in half)
- Psalm 34:8 "Taste & See" verse or the weekly memory verse printed (optional: printed on labels)

Instructions:

1. Use a sharp knife to carefully cut your chosen citrus fruits (lemons, limes, oranges, or grapefruit) in half, making sure the cut is as straight as possible.
2. Place a small amount of paint on a plate—one plate for each color. Kids can share the colors if needed.
3. Dip the cut side of the fruit into the paint, then gently press it onto the cardstock to create a stamp. Remember, a little paint goes a long way and encourage them not to "paint" with the fruit like a brush—just stamp it.
4. Allow the paper to dry completely before hanging up and enjoying the vibrant, fruity artwork!
5. Add the printed label or write the verse on the paper.

Activity/Snack: Taste and See[15]

Purchase assorted chocolates (a box of mixed chocolates works well) or a selection of fruits the children may have never tried before. Be creative and choose foods that might not look appealing on the outside but are surprisingly good on the inside. Seasonal fruits are always a great option, and visiting an international market can help you find unique and exotic fruits.

Place the items you've chosen in the center of the table or on a counter. Before they sample anything, ask the children, "What do you think this will taste like?"

Discuss how, just like with food, we can't truly know what something is like without examining it closely, smelling it, and then tasting it.

God is like this. Just as we can't fully understand what a new food tastes like until we experience it, we can't fully know God without drawing close to Him. He invites us to "taste and see" His goodness.

How can we experience God's goodness? By reading His Word, praying, being filled with the Holy Spirit, and looking for His presence in our everyday lives.

After the children taste the treat, ask, "Now that you've tasted this, would you share it with a friend?" Once we experience the goodness of God, we naturally want to share it with others.

Let each child choose another treat to share with someone else.

I brought a dragon fruit for the children to try. I had never tasted it myself, so it was a new experience for all of us. The outside of the fruit could be considered beautiful because it is vibrant and colorful, but the inside is unexpected, and the taste is quite bland. None of the children seemed to

---

[15]Adapted from "The Fruit of the Spirit… Goodness…", 2020, The City Church, (https://www.thecitychurch.org.uk/city-kids-goodness). Adapted with permission. Permission granted on March 7, 2025.

enjoy it, but it was a great opportunity to explain that while it wasn't their favorite, some people find it delicious. For those who like it, it's a real treat, just as some people experience God's goodness in different ways.

Activity

Your grandkids like ours probably enjoy hiking or taking a walk in the woods. Use this time as a wonderful opportunity to teach lessons drawn from creation. As you hike together, talk openly about how you see God's goodness in the world around you. Share your observations about nature—whether it's the beauty of the trees or the songs of the birds—and point out how all of it reflects God's goodness.

Reflections

Looking back on this week of Grandkids Camp, I was reminded of how little ones think—especially by our youngest grandchild, who was almost three. On the first night, as the other children lined up to receive their blessing from PaQ, he stood off to the side, watching intently as PaQ laid his hands on each child and proclaimed Numbers 6:24–26 over them. When they were all finished, he walked up and stood in front of PaQ with a big smile on his face. PaQ asked him, "What do you want?" And with pure, childlike innocence, he replied, "A motorcycle."

Faithfulness

Introduction

This year marked the 8th year of Grandkids Camp held in 2025; we had 6 children ages 3-9. It did get easier as they got older and could do more for themselves such as shower, get dressed, etc. We also had two additional grandkids added to our family so in a couple of years, there will be eight children participating and hopefully more in years to come.

Faithfulness is the quality of being true to one's word, commitments, or beliefs. It is the unwavering commitment and trust in God even when there are challenges in life.

It involves honoring the promises we make and remaining loyal to those we care about. In the Bible, David, the psalmist, often reflects on God's faithfulness, especially in how God keeps His promises without fail.

Faithfulness also means putting others first—being loyal to family, friends, and loved ones. It's about trusting that when we stay faithful, we honor God and allow Him to work in our lives, guiding us, and providing for our needs.

Most importantly, God is faithful. This means He always keeps His promises and does exactly what He says He will do. When we trust in His faithfulness, we can be sure that He will never let us down.

Song: "Great is thy Faithfulness" – Lyrics by Thomas Obediah Chisholm

Memory Verse: Lamentations 3:22-23

"*The steadfast love of the Lord never ceases; His mercies never come to an end; they are new every morning; great is your faithfulness*."

Faithfulness: Day One

Bible Story: 1 Samuel 19-23—Jonathan and David are Faithful Friends
Read 1 Samuel 19-23, especially chapter 20 or paraphrase the story in your own words.

Introduction Question:

1. Do you remember the story of David and Goliath? (I'm sure many of you do!) David, the young shepherd boy who defeated the giant with just a sling and a stone is the same David we're talking about here.

Story Introduction:

David was a faithful servant of God. After defeating Goliath, he became a hero, and King Saul, Jonathan's father, initially liked David. But then something changed. King Saul grew jealous of David because people began to celebrate David's victories in battle. First Samuel 18:12 says, *"Saul was afraid of David because the Lord was with him."* Saul's jealousy turned into hatred, and eventually, he wanted to kill David.

So, David was forced to run away. But even in this difficult time, he had a loyal friend— Jonathan, Saul's son. Jonathan and David's friendship is a beautiful example of faithfulness, even when things are hard. Jonathan chose to stay true to David, even though his father wanted to harm him. In 1 Samuel 20, we see how Jonathan risked his own life to warn David of Saul's plans and help him escape. Jonathan's loyalty to David was stronger than his loyalty to his own father.

Discussion Questions:

1. How would you feel if your best friend's father was so angry with you that he wanted to get rid of you—maybe even kill you?
2. How would you feel about your best friend's father after that? Would you still respect him? Would you still show him kindness?
3. What would this situation do to your friendship? Would you still trust your best friend? Would you stay friends even in the face of all this conflict?
4. How would you feel if your best friend risked his/her life to save yours—especially if doing so made his/her own father even angrier?
5. Who do you think had it harder—David or Jonathan?
6. Who else showed a beautiful friendship to sinners? Jesus. He loves us even when we are not loyal and sin against Him by doing bad things, and He even died for our sins. We can have this beautiful friendship with Him if we believe in Him and believe that He died for our sins and submit our lives to be faithful to follow Him.

Reflections:

Sometimes in life, you might find yourself in situations like David, where things seem unfair or difficult. It's during those times that having a friend like Jonathan—someone who is loyal and faithful no matter the cost—makes all the difference. Jesus can be that true friend. Other times, you may find yourself in the position of Jonathan, standing by and supporting a friend who needs you, even if it's hard or risky, and you can share with them about Jesus.

Remember, true friends are the ones who are faithful to you no matter what happens. And not just friends—your family, like brothers, sisters, or cousins, can be your best friends too. It's all about being faithful to each other, just like David and Jonathan were faithful to one another, and Jesus is faithful to those who put their trust in Him.

Activity: Friends Stick Close Race

Have your grandchildren participate in a three-legged race.

Supplies:

- Bandanas or sacks/pillowcases

Instructions:

1. Pair them up based on size so each child has a partner who is about the same height.
2. Use bandanas to tie one leg of each pair together, requiring them to cooperate as they run or walk to the finish line. Alternatively, you can have them each put one leg into a sack or an old pillowcase and hold it up as they move together.
3. Line them up at the starting point and point them toward the finish line.
4. Remind your grandchildren that a true friend is always there to help, especially when things get challenging. Encourage them to support each other, slow down if needed, and cheer one another on. Make it clear that unkind or discouraging words aren't allowed. You can even join in as a grandparent to model how to work together and show kindness.

Activity: Friends Obstacle Course

Supplies (Possible Ideas):

- Chairs or tables to crawl under
- 2 X 4 for balance beam or jumping over
- Blocks of wood to climb over
- Tossing a ball into a basket or corn hole toss

Set up an obstacle course indoors or outdoors, depending on the weather, and make sure it's age-appropriate for your grandchildren. Use arrows or numbers to guide the children through the course in the correct order. Include a variety of activities like climbing, crawling, jumping, or anything else you know they'll enjoy.

Pair the children up with a sibling or cousin, ideally matching the oldest with the youngest, so each pair can help one another. Remind them that the goal isn't just to finish quickly—it's to finish together, helping and encouraging each other along the way. Let them know they can't move on to the next challenge until both teammates have completed the current one.

Encourage the kids to support one another by offering kind words, letting their partner go first, or even lending a hand when an obstacle is especially tough.

If you want to make it competitive, use a stopwatch to time each pair and see how fast they can complete the course. But if you'd rather keep it cooperative, simply focus on having them finish as quickly as they can while still working as a team.

While some children are waiting their turn, encourage them to cheer on their siblings or cousins with kind and motivating words.

This fun activity is all about working together and being faithful to your partner.

Craft: Friendship Bracelets

Supplies:

- Beads in various colors
- Letter beads to spell names or words like "faithful," "friend," or "love"
- String for making bracelets (I used leftover beads and string from Grandkids Camp – Peace.)

Instructions:

There are several fun ways you can approach this craft. One option is to have each child create a bracelet to give to someone special. Another idea is to let them make two identical bracelets—one to keep and one to give to a friend as a symbol of faithfulness. A third option is to divide the beads by color and give each child a bag of beads in a different color. To complete their friendship bracelet, they'll need to share their beads with one another.

This activity requires very little instruction for you to provide. Your role is to guide the children as they share, trade, and communicate to get the colors they need. Sharing and communication are key to building strong friendships, and this craft offers a great opportunity for them to practice both. Encourage them as they ask for beads or offer some of their own in exchange.

As you work with them, you might take a moment to talk about the friendship and faithfulness between Jonathan and David in the Bible. Just like they had to communicate and ask for help, the children can support each other by sharing their beads—or even giving some away without being asked.

And anytime you need help with anything in life, you can always turn to Jesus. You can pray and ask Him for help, because apart from Him, you can do nothing. This craft isn't just fun—it's a meaningful way to help kids understand what it means to be a faithful friend.

Craft: Friendship Tree

Supplies:

- Large piece of paper, poster board, or brown wrapping paper
- Markers
- Various colors of finger paints
- Plates or pie pans for paint

Instructions:

Start by drawing the outline of a tree on the large piece of paper. At the base of the tree, write “Faithful Friends” in big, bold letters. Prepare the finger paints by pouring different colors onto plates or pie pans. Then, have each child take turns dipping their hand into the paint and adding a handprint as a "leaf" on the tree. They can also add handprints at the base of the tree, and you might consider writing their names next to the prints on the ground—they’ll love seeing their names included!

Once everyone has added a handprint, give them the opportunity to take another turn so the tree fills up as much as you like. This becomes a fun and interactive way for the children to see how they are all part of the tree of "faithful friends."

When the tree is complete, display it proudly throughout Grandkids Camp. Be sure to take a picture of the artwork to share with the parents—since the tree won’t be able to go home with the children, the photo will let them see the beautiful work they've created!

Snack: Friendship Snack

Before the camp, ask parents to have their children choose a favorite snack to share. These snacks should not be single serving size but rather full-size pre-packaged snack items. Let them know they'll need to bring at least one cup of their chosen snack for the special treat we'll be making. Snack options could include things like pretzels, popcorn, goldfish, fruit snacks, cereal, dried fruits (like raisins), marshmallows, mini candies, and more. It's also a good idea to have a few extra snacks on hand in case any of the children forget to bring theirs.

Place all the snacks into a large bowl, with each child adding one cup of their chosen snack. Mix everything together, then scoop out a cup of the "Friendship Snack" for each child to enjoy!

Faithfulness: Day Two

Bible Story: Matthew 25:13-30—The Parable of the Talents

Discussion Questions:

1. What are talents?
   Talents are the gifts and abilities that God has given to each of us. It is also God's truth being given to us as a gift. Some people may excel at sports: others at memorizing things, crafting, singing, cooking, listening, or even offering a helping hand. Everyone has special talents that God has uniquely provided for them to use to bring Him glory.
2. What is Jesus teaching us about using our talents?
   Jesus teaches that when we use the talents God has given us, He will bless us and give us more. The more we faithfully use our gifts, the more God will trust us with. God gives us talents so we can serve others and spread the love of Jesus so His kingdom will grow, not for us to grow our own kingdom or riches.
3. What is the greatest gift that God offers to you?
   Just like talents are gifts and not earned, salvation from our sins is a free gift that God offers to everyone. It is not something you earn.
4. What happens to those who don't use their talents?
   If we choose to "bury" our talents, by not using them, we risk losing them altogether. Just as in the parable, the servant who buried his talent had it taken away. When we don't use our abilities, we don't grow, and the potential of our gifts fades away.

God wants us to be faithful and share the love of Jesus and the gift of salvation with others.

5. Why does God give us talents?
   God entrusts us with talents because we are valuable to Him. These gifts aren't just for us—they are meant to be used for His glory and for the good of others. If we choose to focus on things like watching TV or playing video games instead of using our talents for God's purposes, we may miss out on the blessings that come from serving Him. Ultimately, God may give those gifts to someone else who is using theirs to honor Him.
6. What if you're not sure what your talents are?
   If you don't yet know what your special talents are, ask your parents or other people who know you well. They might be able to help you recognize your gifts. Pay attention to the things you enjoy and that others compliment you on—this can be a clue to the talents God has given you. Even the smallest gift is important in God's eyes. And if you use what He has given you, He will help it grow and use it for His glory.
7. Encouraging Others:

   Take time to notice and encourage others by pointing out the gifts you see in them. It could be something as simple as how they help around the house, their creativity, or their kindness. When you encourage someone, you're reminding them of the special ability God has given them. You might even notice talents in others that they don't see in themselves!

Grandparents' Role:

This is also a wonderful opportunity for grandparents to encourage their grandchildren. Share with them the talents you see in them, whether it's their kindness, creativity, giving hugs, enjoying cooking, or even their willingness to help. When you affirm and praise their gifts, you're not only showing love, but you're helping them understand that these talents are special and given by God. Encourage them in how they may be able to use them to show the love of Jesus to others.

Remember, no matter how small or simple a talent may seem, it is special to God and can make a big difference when used for His glory.

Object Lesson: Cutting the Corners Activity

Take a piece of paper and ask your grandchild to count the four corners. Then, carefully ask one child to cut off one corner with a pair of scissors and give it to you. Explain that sometimes, we try to keep things for ourselves, but when we give away what God has given us, He blesses us with more.

Next, ask another child to count the corners again. You'll notice that there are now five corners. Continue the activity by having each of the four original corners cut off by a different child. Each time a corner is given away, the child will gain an extra one.

Use this activity to share an important lesson: One of the greatest gifts God has given us is the good news about Jesus. It is available to everyone, and just like with the corners, when we are faithful to share the good news with others, His kingdom can grow, and we are blessed.

Craft/Object Lesson: Offering Our Gifts to God

Supplies:

- Index cards
- Wrapping paper
- Markers
- Glue
- Scissors

Instructions:

1. Give each child an index card.

2. Have them cut a piece of wrapping paper to fit one side of the card, then glue it on like a gift wrapping.
3. On the blank side, ask each child to write down a talent or gift they have—or something they believe they're good at.
4. Once they've written it down, have them fold the card in half like a greeting card.

Discussion & Prayer:

Talk with the kids about how every gift we have comes from God and how we can use those gifts to honor Him. Ask: *Would you like to use your talent to serve God?*

Then, invite the children to say a short prayer, offering their talent to God. Lead by example — create your own card and share a simple prayer out loud. This will help guide them in how to talk to God about their gifts.

One of the grandchildren left his card so I had the opportunity to read what he had written. It touched my heart with him wanting to give God his mouth and asking God to help speak words that would tell others about Jesus.

Purpose:

This lesson can be used to encourage your grandchildren to recognize the unique talents God has given them and inspire them to use those gifts for His glory.

Craft: Coins[16]

For this craft, you can use premade modeling clay for ease, but if you're feeling creative, you can try making your own porcelain clay with this

[16] Adapted from "How will you use your talents?" by Tricia Messing, 2017, Adventures in a Messy Life, (https://ticiamessing.com/parable-talents-lesson/). Adapted with permission. Permission granted by author on March 4, 2025.

simple recipe. Each batch will make 5-8 coins, depending on how large the children make each coin.

Supplies:

- 1 microwavable cup for each child
- 2 tablespoons baking soda
- 1 tablespoon cornstarch
- 1.5 tablespoons water
- Paints (for decoration)
- Optional: Biscuit cutters (for shaping)
- Modeling clay (as an alternative to the homemade recipe)

Instructions:

1. **For Homemade Clay**: Mix the baking soda, cornstarch, and water together in a bowl. Microwave the mixture for 15 seconds at a time, stirring after each interval. Continue until the mixture thickens to the consistency of dough. Let it cool down before using, as it will be too sticky when hot.
2. **Shaping the Coins**: Once the dough has cooled, have the children roll it into small balls and shape them into flat coins. You can also use small biscuit cutters to make them perfectly round. Don't flatten them too much, or they will break more easily once hard.
3. **Baking**: If you made the homemade clay, bake the coins at 175°F for 30-45 minutes. They're ready for painting once they've cooled completely. For modeling clay, simply shape the coins without baking, but they will need time to dry out (overnight works best).
4. **Painting**: After the coins have cooled or dried, let the children paint their coins with fun designs.
5. **Name the Coins:** Let the children name each coin for a talent they have.

Bonus Activity: While the coins are baking or drying, the children can make a matching coin bag to keep their creations in!

The coins can represent talents or the sharing of the good news with others. When we keep the good news to ourselves, the kingdom of God will not grow.

Crafts: Coin Purse Craft

This simple and fun coin purse craft will give the children a chance to create a personalized pouch to store their handmade coins!

Supplies:

- 12" x 12" squares of fabric (one for each child)
- Yarn or heavy string
- Scissors
- Tape
- Hole punch (or scissors for cutting slits)

Instructions:

1. **Prepare the Fabric**: Punch holes around the edges of the fabric square, leaving a small space between each hole. Make sure the holes aren't too close to the edge so the fabric doesn't tear. If the hole punch doesn't work, you can simply cut small slits instead. Children may need help with this part.
2. **Prepare the Yarn**: Give each child a long piece of yarn. Tape one end of the yarn to make a point, so it can be used like a needle for threading.
3. **Sewing the Purse**: Show the children how to thread the yarn through the holes, starting at one corner. They should go in through one hole and back up through the next, continuing this process all the way around the fabric square.
4. **Finishing the Coin Purse**: Once they've sewn all the way around, there should be enough yarn at both ends to pull the fabric edges together. Help the children tie the yarn tightly, closing the fabric into a pouch shape.

5. **Enjoy**: The children can now use their coin purses to store their clay coins or other small treasures!

Talent Time/Show

Instructions:

1. **Introduction:** Start by asking each child to share something they feel they're good at. Encourage them to think about both big and small talents—whether it's drawing, singing, acting, dancing, or even something quieter like solving puzzles or making people laugh. Make sure each child shares at least one talent.
2. **Explaining the talent show:** Once you have everyone's list, tell the children they'll have a chance to show their talents to the group. Remind them that their talent doesn't have to involve speaking or performing in front of others—it could be drawing a picture, building something with blocks, or even showing a special skill, like tying a knot. Give them time to prepare.
3. **Encouraging participation:** Some children might feel nervous about performing in front of others. Focus on creating a supportive and low-pressure environment. Explain that the goal is to celebrate the gifts God has given them, and that this talent show is a fun way to share those gifts.
4. **Addressing hesitations:** When a child feels reluctant to share, gently remind them of the parable of the talents (Matthew 25:14-30). Explain that hiding their talent out of fear is like burying it, and when they choose to share what they've been given, they're showing faithfulness—and God can use that in even greater ways.
5. **Leading by example:** Be sure to share your own talent, too! Whether it's telling a story, singing a song, or doing something creative, show the children that sharing your gifts is both fun and rewarding. Your example will encourage them to do the same.

6. **Sharing and Celebrating:** Invite each child to present their talent to the group. Celebrate each effort, no matter how big or small, and encourage the group to cheer for each other's abilities.

This "Talent Time" is a great way to build confidence, foster creativity, and remind children that their unique talents are gifts from God that should be shared and developed! Our grandchildren share their own unique talents—drawing, songwriting, strength, and helping others. We were deeply moved by the enthusiasm with which each of them took part.

Snack: Chocolate Coins

If you have any grandchildren who enjoy cooking or show an interest in it, give them the opportunity to prepare a snack for everyone using the ingredients you have on hand. This can be a fun way to include their cooking talent in the "Talent Time" show!

Make sure to provide adult supervision as needed, especially if the children are younger or will be using kitchen tools or appliances.

Here's a simple idea to get you started: **Chocolate Coins.** These can be both a treat and a craft that ties into the theme of talents and creativity. If you'd rather not make them from scratch, you can purchase chocolate coins and offer them as a snack instead.

Supplies:

- Chocolate chips or any type of melting chocolate (dark, milk, or white)
- Wax paper or parchment paper
- A spoon or small cookie scoop
- Optional: Gold dust or edible glitter (to make them look more like "golden" coins!)

Instructions for Chocolate Coins:

1. **Melting the Chocolate**: If an older child is taking the lead, show them how to safely melt the chocolate. You can use a microwave in short bursts, stirring in between, or melt it using a double boiler on the stove.
2. **Shaping the Coins**: Once the chocolate is melted, let the child spoon small amounts of chocolate onto the wax or parchment paper. They can use a spoon to form them into coin-sized rounds or even use a cookie cutter for the perfect shape.
3. **Optional Decoration**: If desired, sprinkle a little edible gold dust or glitter on top of the coins for a fun, shiny effect!
4. **Setting the Coins**: Let the chocolate coins cool and harden. You can speed up this process by placing them in the refrigerator for 10-15 minutes.
5. **Enjoy**: Once they've cooled and hardened, the chocolate coins are ready to enjoy! They can even be wrapped in foil or placed in a little bag to resemble real coins.

If cooking isn't their talent but the children still want to participate, perhaps they can help decorate or pass out the coins during the talent time. This snack would be a perfect addition to the "Talent Show" where everyone can enjoy the homemade treat!

Faithfulness: Day Three

Bible Story: Daniel 3:1-30—Shadrach, Meshach, and Abednego

Before diving into this powerful story, it's important to understand the context. This story is about three Jewish men—Shadrach, Meshach, and Abednego—who were taken from their homeland to serve in the Babylonian empire. In this new, foreign land, they were forced to adapt to the empire's laws and its worship of many gods, yet their devotion to the one true God remained unchanged. Like any faithful person, their faith was tested in a very real way.

Discussion Questions:

1. Would you have the courage to stand firm for God if you were faced with the threat of death, just like Shadrach, Meshach, and Abednego?
2. Do you think it would be easier to stand up with faithfulness if you had friends standing by your side, like these men did?

Reflections:

We live in a time where our faithfulness is or will be tested. We may not face such life-and-death situations, but our faith is still tested in many ways. In some parts of the world, following God comes with real, physical risks—just like it did for these three men.

There may come a time when we have to decide: Will we stand for God, or will we bow to the pressures of the world? Will we choose God's way, or our own comfort and safety? This is a difficult decision, and it can feel like the heat is turning up—just as it did for Shadrach, Meshach, and Abednego.

But the good news is this: When we stand for God, He stands with us. As Isaiah 43:2-3 promises, *"When you pass through the waters, I will be with you; and when you walk through the fire, you will not be burned, for I am the Lord your God."* God was with Shadrach, Meshach, and Abednego in the fiery furnace, and He will be with us in our trials too. God is faithful.

Craft: Glowing Campfire

This craft is a fun and creative way to bring the story of Shadrach, Meshach, and Abednego to life. The glowing campfire will remind the children of how God protected the three men in the fiery furnace. Here's how to make your very own glowing campfire!

Supplies:

- Clear plastic cup
- Tissue paper in red, orange, and yellow
- Glue (such as Tacky glue)
- LED tea light
- Twig or thin craft stick
- Cotton balls
- Brown construction paper
- Scissors

Instructions:

1. **Prepare the Tissue Paper:** Cut or tear the tissue paper into small pieces.
2. **Create the Fire Effect:** Lightly scrunch up the tissue paper pieces and glue them to the outside of the clear plastic cup. Cover the whole cup, layering the colors red, orange, and yellow to resemble a flame.
3. **Add the Logs:** While the tissue paper dries, glue a cotton ball to the end of a thin craft stick or twig to act as a "marshmallow." Then, cut strips of brown construction paper to create logs for the campfire. You can add details to the logs with markers or crayons, making them look like real wood.
4. **Assemble the Campfire:** Glue the logs together in a pattern that will hold the cup securely on top.

5. **Light It Up:** Place the LED tea light on the logs and set the cup upside down over the tea light. In a dark room, the campfire will glow just like a real fire!

After dinner, we had a campfire to roast marshmallows and reflected on how intense that fire must have been for Shadrach, Meshach, and Abednego. As we enjoyed the warmth of the fire, we also talked about how God sent an angel to protect the three men in the flames. It's a great way to connect the story to our own experiences and remember how God was with them, just as He is with us in our own trials.

Snack Idea: Smoked Snacks

For a fun and thematic snack, you can serve a variety of smoked treats to tie into the story of Shadrach, Meshach, and Abednego in the fiery furnace. These snacks will remind everyone of the intense heat of the fire they faced and the protection they received from God. Here are some smoked snack ideas to get creative with:

- **Slim Jims** or **Beef Jerky** – These provide a great meaty, smoky flavor that's sure to be a hit with the kids.
- **Smoked Cheetos** – A fun twist on the classic Cheetos, these will add a smoky, spicy snack to the mix.
- **Smoked Salmon** – For something a little more sophisticated, smoked salmon is a flavorful option.
- **Smoked Nuts** – Try smoked almonds, cashews, or peanuts for a crunchy, savory treat.
- **Smoked Cheese** – If you want to get a little fancier, smoked cheese like Gouda or cheddar can be a fun addition.

You can get as creative as you like with finding any smoked foods—this is your chance to experiment and give your snack table a unique and flavorful twist!

Faithfulness: Day Four

Today, I listed more crafts and activities than you may have time to use, so choose the ones that you feel your grandchildren will enjoy the most.

Bible Story: Numbers 13–14—Joshua and Caleb

Let's dive into the story of Joshua and Caleb, two men who demonstrated incredible faith in God when the Israelites were on the brink of entering the Promised Land. This land, flowing with milk and honey, was promised to them by God after they were freed from slavery in Egypt. But before they could take possession of it, Moses sent twelve spies to scout the land. Ten of the spies came back with a negative report, focusing on the giants they saw in the land and the challenges they would face. But two men, Joshua and Caleb, trusted in God's promises and urged the people to move forward in faith.

Read the following passages from Numbers 13 and 14 (13:1-3, 16b-14:12, 14:24, 14:27-30, 14:38).

Discussion Questions:

1. What food did the spies find when they explored the land?
   They found grapes so large that it took two men to carry a single cluster on a pole! The land was abundant with good food—just as God had promised.
2. Who showed faith in God?
   Joshua and Caleb showed faith in God. While the other spies were afraid, Joshua and Caleb trusted that God would help them conquer the land.
3. How did Joshua and Caleb show their faithfulness to God?
   They showed faithfulness by believing God when He promised them the land. Despite the challenges, they were willing to obey God and trust that He would give them the victory.
4. What did Joshua and Caleb want to do?

They wanted to enter the land and fight for it, confident that God would give them the strength to overcome the giants and take possession of the land.

5. Why were the other spies afraid to go into the land flowing with milk and honey?
   The other spies were afraid because they saw that the people in the land were giants, and they felt small and powerless, like grasshoppers compared to them. They focused on their fears and the challenges instead of trusting in God's promise.
6. Did Joshua and Caleb see the same things the other spies saw? Why was their response different?
   Yes, Joshua and Caleb saw the same giants and challenges as the other spies, but their response was different. They focused on God's faithfulness and His promises, while the others focused on the obstacles. Joshua and Caleb believed that God was bigger than the giants in the land.
7. What does it mean to have faith in God?
   Having faith in God means believing that God is almighty and trusting that when He tells us to do something, He will give us the strength to do it. It means relying on His faithfulness, even when we face difficult circumstances. Most importantly, having faith in God is believing that He loves us and has a wonderful plan for our lives. But our sin has separated us from God so that we cannot know or experience His love and plan for our lives. God sent Jesus to take the punishment for our sins by dying for us. He did this so we can have a relationship with God and experience His love and plan. But each of us must choose to believe or have faith in what Jesus did and turn from our sins to follow and obey Jesus. We receive Jesus into our life and hear by faith; that is ultimate faith in God. When we believe and trust in God, He will always be faithful to us.

For more or extended lesson for older children, go to - https://www.crosswalk.com/faith/spiritual-life/lessons-we-can-learn-about-faith-from-joshua-and-caleb.html

Craft: Spy Glasses

To tie in with the story of the spies in the Promised Land, make your very own spy glasses! These fun, creative binoculars will help the kids imagine themselves as spies, just like Joshua and Caleb, scouting out the land.

Supplies:

- One empty paper towel roll per child (or two toilet paper rolls to make binoculars)
- Colorful duct tape or washi tape (craft stores have a variety of fun colors and patterns)
- Tape or glue
- Yarn or string (to make a strap for wearing the spy glasses around their neck)

Instructions:

1. **Decorate the Spy Glasses:**
   Start by decorating the outside of the roll(s) with colorful tape. You can cover the entire roll with one color or use different patterns to make it look like a true spy tool. Let the kids get creative!
   a. For the paper towel roll, you'll have one large spyglass (like a pirate's spyglass).
   b. For binoculars, use two toilet paper rolls. After decorating, place the rolls side by side and use glue or tape to secure them together.
2. **Add a Strap:**
   Once the spyglass or binoculars are assembled, attach a piece of yarn or string to each side. This will allow the kids to wear their spy glasses around their neck, just like real spies!

3. **Enjoy Your Spy Glasses:**
   Now they're ready to wear their spy glasses and imagine they're scouting out the land, just like the spies in the story of Joshua and Caleb. You can even encourage them to use their new spy glasses while asking questions or discussing the story!

This craft is a great way to bring the story to life, and the kids will love wearing their spy glasses as they remember how Joshua and Caleb stood firm in their faith!

Crafts: Fingerpaint Clusters of Grapes

To help the children connect with the part of the story where the spies bring back a huge cluster of grapes, create a fun and colorful craft. This fingerpaint activity will allow them to imagine what it was like for the spies to carry such large grapes back to the Israelites.

Supplies:

- White paper – 1 sheet per child
- Purple fingerpaint (for the grapes)
- Green and brown markers (for the leaves and stick)
- Pencil (for outlining)

Instructions:

1. **Draw the Stick:**
   Have the children use a brown marker (or pencil first, then trace over with a marker) to draw a stick or pole at the top of their paper. Explain that the spies used this stick to carry the large bunch of grapes, just like the ones they saw in the Promised Land.
2. **Outline the Grape Cluster:**
   Help the children draw a rough outline of a grape cluster just below the stick. This doesn't need to be perfect—just a simple shape to represent where the grapes will go.
3. **Fingerpaint the Grapes:**

Using purple fingerpaint, let the children dip their fingers or thumbs into the paint and gently press them onto the paper to create the grapes. Encourage them to use different amounts of paint for different sizes of grapes, creating a natural, clustered look.

4. **Add Leaves:**
   Using a green marker (or fingerpaint), children can add a couple of green leaves at the top of the cluster, near the stick. This will make it look even more like a real bunch of grapes.
5. **Optional – Add the Spies:**
   For older children or those who enjoy drawing, they can use a brown marker to draw **two** men carrying the stick—one on each end of the pole. This adds an extra level of detail to the craft and reinforces the idea of how big the grapes were.
6. **Finish the Craft:**
   Allow the crafts to dry and then talk to the children about how these grapes were so large that it took two men to carry them, just like in the Bible story when the spies returned from the land of Canaan.

This activity is a fun and tactile way to engage with the story of the spies in the Promised Land and helps children connect with the theme of faith, trust, and God's promises!

Craft

If you have older children, they might find this craft more appealing than fingerpainting, though kids of all ages will enjoy it. Why not combine both activities? Use the twigs and leaves for the structure and let the kids fingerpaint the grapes. Alternatively, they could collect small stones or use purple pom-poms for the grapes.

Supplies:

- Sturdy cardboard
- Craft or tacky glue

- Twigs
- Leaves
- Small stones (or purple pom-poms from a craft store)
- Purple paint

Instructions:

1. First, have the children arrange the twigs and leaves to create a grapevine or to represent the sticks used by the spies used to carry the grapes.
2. Underneath, they can form one or two grape clusters, using either purple pom-poms or small stones (which will need to be painted purple).
3. Use tacky glue to secure everything in place.

This craft can be done after an "I Spy" nature walk, where kids can collect twigs, sticks, and leaves to incorporate into their project.

Snack

So many delicious options inspired by the story!

You can offer a variety of fruits like grapes, pomegranates, and figs, along with milk and honey. It's a fun opportunity for children to try something new that they might not have tasted before. If figs aren't available or you'd prefer something simpler, Fig Newtons are a great alternative.

Another idea is to make a refreshing fruit salad. Add a bit of sweetened condensed milk to give it a creamy, sweet flavor, especially if you're using tart fruits. For a natural touch of sweetness, drizzle a little honey over the top.

Activity: I Spy

This game is a great way for your grandkids to use their new spy glasses from the craft project! If you've never played "I Spy," it's a simple and fun activity. Choose one person to take on the role of the "spy" and have them say, “I spy with my little eye something that is (name a color),” while secretly picking an object in the room that matches that color. Then, the other children take turns guessing what the object is. The one who guesses correctly gets to be the next spy.

To make it even more fun, the kids can use the spy glasses they made as part of the craft to pretend they’re searching for clues or objects around the room!

Activity: Nature Walk & "I Spy" Adventure

Take the kids on a fun outdoor walk where they can continue to play "I Spy" while searching for specific items in nature. Encourage them to bring their new spyglasses or binoculars to help them find things on their list. You can print out a sheet for each child with the items they need to look for during the walk. They can either collect the items (if safe to do so) or simply check them off as they spot them.

For younger children who can’t read yet, consider printing out pictures of the items they should look for. You can adapt the list based on your location and the season. Here’s a suggested list of things they can search for:

- Bird
- Owl or Eagle
- Pinecone
- Rabbit or squirrel
- Moss
- Rock
- Nest
- Ladybug
- Grasshopper
- Butterfly
- Green grass
- Bumblebee

- Spiderweb
- Tree stump
- Feather
- Berries
- Acorn
- Wildflower
- Dragonfly
- Brown grass
- Ant
- Water
- Wooden sign
- Fern
- Stick
- Mushrooms
- Worm
- Trees

- Animal footprints
- Caterpillar
- Snail
- Bug
- Cloud
- Fallen tree
- Frog, toad, or lizard
- Fish

Reflection: After I had handed out the printed sheets for each child, along with a pencil to mark off their items, one of the younger children asked, "Can I have a clipboard?" Now I hadn't thought of this, so I had to come up with a quick plan. We had just finished cutting up pieces of cardboard for another activity, so I gave each of the children a piece of cardboard and taped their sheet to it as their "clipboard." This did make it easier for them to mark off each item.

Wrap up:

As always, at the end of Grandkids Camp, be sure to take a moment to review the verses the children have learned throughout the week. This is a great opportunity to celebrate their progress and help reinforce what they've absorbed. Record them reciting the verses for the parents so they can see what their child has accomplished and continue to support their learning at home. It's a wonderful way to close out the camp experience and encourage kids to keep practicing and memorizing!

Gentleness

Introduction

These lessons are still being developed, as we have not yet hosted Grandkids Camp for this theme. We will again have 6 grandchildren attend, with ages from 4-10 years. We are continuing with the "Fruit of the Spirit" theme, as each of these fruits is essential in our lives and helps point the grandchildren to their need for Jesus. We cannot produce these fruits apart from Him.

This year, we also plan to introduce Bible journaling to the older children. We will provide grandchildren with a journal and teach them how to spend time each morning reflecting on the Bible verse of the week, writing down how it applies to them or what they have learned so far.

Defined: Gentleness is often linked to kindness, but it goes deeper, reflecting a softness of heart and a compassionate attitude toward others. It is the quality of being kind, tender, mild-mannered, and calm, with a genuine desire to help, even when others may have wronged you. At its core, gentleness is about responding with kindness and understanding, creating an atmosphere of warmth and care.

God shows gentleness through compassion and forgiveness. Gentleness is not weakness but strength under control. Jesus is the best example of this type of gentleness.

Song: "Gentle Jesus" by Charles Wesley

Memory Verse: Proverbs 15:1 (NASB)

"*A gentle answer turns away wrath, But a harsh word stirs up anger*."

Gentleness: Day One

Start the day by discussing the meaning of gentleness. It's a great opportunity to ask them what they think it means—you might be surprised by how much they already understand. Sometimes, they know more than we give them credit for!

Bible Story: John 8:1-11 (*The Message Bible*)—Casting the First Stone

Adultery can be a difficult concept to explain to young children, but it's important to approach the topic in a way they can understand. You might want to start by asking if they've heard the word "adultery" before and let them lead the conversation. If they don't know what it means, you can explain it simply.

- Adultery is when someone doesn't keep their marriage promises.
- Or adultery is when someone acts like another person is their husband or wife, even though they already have one.

Discussion Questions:

1. Who was gentle in the story?
2. Who was not gentle?
3. Was this a gentle or harsh way to point out sin

4. Do you think the woman would have learned to love Jesus if He had thrown stones at her?
5. Would you have thrown stones?
6. When Jesus said, *"Let him who is without sin cast the first stone,"* who was without sin? (Answer: Only Jesus.)
7. How did Jesus show gentleness? He didn't respond with harshness or meanness. Instead, He led with compassion, showing us how to treat others gently when they sin, even when they have sinned against us.
8. Does Jesus show this same gentleness to us? How? This story is a powerful reminder of how Jesus calls us to act with gentleness and mercy, especially when others fall short or hurt us.

Craft/Activity: Balloon Stress Ball

Supplies:

- Heavy-duty balloons (Choose the strongest balloons you can find)
- Flour or soft sand
- Funnel
- Permanent Marker
- Scoop
- Pen or pencil (to help push down the filling)

Instructions:

1. **Prepare the Balloon:** Give each child a balloon. Start by blowing it up slightly to stretch it out, making it easier to fill.
2. **Fill the Balloon:** Place the funnel into the opening of the balloon. Help the children scoop the flour or soft sand into the funnel to fill the balloon. You can also tap the balloon gently to help the contents settle, or use a pen or pencil to push the flour/sand in.
3. **Seal the Balloon:** Once the balloon is filled, tie the end tightly and cut off any excess balloon to avoid any loose ends.

4. **Decorate the Balloon:** Use a permanent marker to write the word "gentleness" or a Bible verse on one side of the balloon. On the other side, the kids can draw a face or design a fun pattern.

How to Use the Stress Ball: Explain to your grandchildren that sometimes, when things don't go your way, you may feel frustrated or upset, and you might not always respond as gently as you should. The balloon stress ball is something you can squeeze to let out your frustration instead of taking it out on others. The verse or the word "gentleness" written on the balloon will remind you to pause, take a deep breath, and ask God to help you be gentle, even when you're feeling upset.

You can use this stress ball whenever you need a moment to calm down or think about how you can choose gentleness in a difficult situation.

Activity: Relay Races

Supplies:

- Balloons - blown up
- Eggs
- Spoons

Tip: Consider doing this activity outside for more space and fun!

Race 1: Place a balloon between your knees. Be careful not to pop it! Keep the balloon in place as you race to the finish line. If the balloon falls out, you must return to the start and try again.

Race 2: Place an egg on a spoon and hold it steady. Your goal is to walk or run to the finish line without dropping the egg or letting it break.

Participants can compete individually or form teams for a relay-style race!

Activity: Water Balloon Toss

Supplies:

- Water balloons

- Bucket
- Hose or sink for filling balloons

Tip: This activity is perfect for a hot summer day outdoors!

Start by filling up the water balloons. If the kids are younger, you might want to fill them in advance, but if they're older, let them help with the filling process—it's part of the fun! Be sure to fill plenty of balloons, as they'll likely want to keep playing after the toss.

Consider having the children change into bathing suits before you begin.

Ground Rules: Set some simple guidelines, like only throwing balloons at people below the waist to keep things safe and fair.

How to Play:

1. Divide the kids into teams of two and have them stand in two rows facing their partner.
2. Begin with the teams standing about two feet apart. The goal is for each team to gently toss the water balloon back and forth without it popping.
3. After every successful toss, each team must take a step back, keeping their lines straight.
4. If a team drops or breaks their balloon, they must sit out and watch the others continue.

Once everyone's balloon has popped, start the game again with fresh balloons! Continue playing as long as everyone's having fun, and be sure grandparents join in the fun, too!

Snack: Soft treat that requires gentleness to avoid bruising or breaking.

Suggestions:

- Tomato – Cherry tomatoes are perfect, since they can be eaten in one bite.

- Mango – A favorite among our grandkids!
- Banana
- Raspberries
- Strawberries

Gentleness: Day Two

Bible Story: 1 Kings 11:43-12:17, Zechariah 9:9 and Matthew 11:28-30—Harsh King Rehoboam and Gentle King Jesus

Introduction:

Today, we're going to compare two kings: one who was harsh and one who was gentle.

Introductions: Rehoboam became king of Israel after his father, Solomon, died. Before Rehoboam, Israel had been ruled by three kings: Saul, David, and Solomon. These were mostly good kings who cared about the people. But Rehoboam's reign was different.

Read 1 Kings 11:43-12:17

Discussion Questions:

1. Did Rehoboam sound like a gentle king?
2. How was King Rehoboam harsh and not gentle?
3. Would you want to serve him? Did the people want to serve him?
4. What kind of king (or queen) would you be?
5. Is Jesus a harsh or gentle king? Why?
6. Who did King Rehoboam listen to?
7. Who does Jesus listen to?
8. Do you think your friends will always tell you the right thing to do?
9. Who is an elder in your life? Someone who is older and wiser?

Comparing King Rehoboam with Gentle Jesus

In this story, Jesus shows His love and kindness to children. The disciples, on the other hand, were arguing about who was the greatest and thought that the children were not important enough to be around Jesus.

Read Zechariah 9:9 and Matthew 11:28-30 and/or "The Friend of Little Children" from the *Jesus Storybook Bible* (page 256).

Discussion Questions:

1. What were the disciples arguing about?
2. How did Jesus show gentleness?
3. What did the disciples want to do with the children?
4. Why did Jesus show gentleness to the children? What point was He trying to make to the disciples and to us? (Jesus was showing that He loves everyone, no matter how young or old, and He wants us to come to Him with trust and joy.)
5. Which king would you prefer to serve and follow, King Rehoboam or Jesus?
6. Have you told Jesus that you want Him to be the King of your life?

Activity: Gentleness vs. Harshness—A Fun Advice Game

In this game, children will decide if the advice or actions you mention are good (gentle) or bad (harsh). Set up two sides of the room:

- Good Advice/Gentleness: Mark one side with a large smiley face.
- Bad Advice/Harshness: Mark the other side with a sad face.

For younger children, use these visual cues to make it easier for them to remember. You can create big signs or place labels on the floor to mark each side clearly.

How to Play:

1. Call out various actions or advice (listed below) and let the children choose which side of the room they think fits best.

2. After each phrase, the children will run to either the Good Advice/Gentleness side or the Bad Advice/Harshness side.
3. Ask them to explain why they chose that side.
4. If a child chooses the wrong side, kindly ask them to explain their reasoning and then discuss why the correct choice is different, helping them understand the distinction between gentleness and harshness.

Examples to Call Out:

- Take the toy away from your friend or sibling – *Harsh*
- Give a hug when someone gets hurt – *Gentleness*
- Play a game with your brother or sister – *Gentleness*
- Push your brother, sister, or cousin away when they are bothering you – *Harsh*
- Yell when you don't get your own way – *Harsh*
- Quietly wait for your lunch or dinner without complaining – *Gentleness*
- Forgiving others – *Gentleness*
- Being angry with someone – *Harsh*
- Hitting someone – *Harsh*
- Giving a back rub – *Gentleness*
- Sharing – *Gentleness*
- Rushing to be first in line – *Harsh*
- Obeying – *Gentleness*
- Telling someone to trip another person – *Bad Advice*
- Telling someone to give a hug – *Good Advice*
- Telling someone to disobey – *Bad Advice*
- Telling someone to share – *Good Advice*

Tips for Success:

After each round, engage the children in a brief discussion to encourage understanding.

Add any challenges or examples your grandchildren may be struggling with to personalize the game!

By the end of the game, the children will better understand the difference between gentle and harsh behaviors, as well as good and bad advice.

Craft: Gentleness Thumbprint

Supplies:

- Large heavy-duty paper or canvas (one for each child)
- Markers or pens
- Ink pads in various colors (or finger paints)
- Frames (optional)

Instructions:

1. **Prepare the word "Gentleness:"**
   Print the word "Gentleness" in large letters across a piece of heavy-duty paper or canvas for each child. You can write it yourself with a marker or use a printed template for easier tracing.
2. **Thumbprint Tracing:**
   Let the children use their fingers or thumbs to "trace" the letters of the word Gentleness by pressing their thumbs onto the paper. They will dip their thumbs into different colored ink pads (or finger paints) and press them onto the lines of the word to fill in the letters.
3. **Creative Freedom:**
   Encourage the children to use different colors for each letter or even combine thumbprints across the letters to make it more colorful and playful.

4. **Optional – Frame the Craft:**
   If you're feeling ambitious, you can frame the artwork after it dries. You can find affordable frames at stores like Wal-Mart or the dollar store to display the kids' creations.

Additional Tips:

If you're using finger paints, be sure to give the children only small amounts to avoid excess mess. This activity allows for creative expression while reinforcing the theme of gentleness through the careful action of thumbprinting.

Once completed, each child will have a personalized piece of art that reflects the theme of gentleness!

Snack: Egg

An egg is delicate, so you need to handle it with gentleness to prevent it from breaking. If you drop it, it will likely crack open, making a mess. Even when frying an egg, you have to be gentle to avoid breaking the yolk. For a snack, you can offer a fried egg or a hard-boiled egg--both are delicious options! It could be fun to teach them how to make deviled eggs.

Activity: Being Gentle[17]

Take an uncooked egg for each of your children and write his or her name on it. Also have them draw a face on the egg. Then place the egg in its own zip-lock bag. Assign each child's egg to a sibling or cousin. Explain that these eggs are fragile and must be handled gently. The children should carry their assigned egg with them during the next hour or two. Set a timer so when it goes off, you can ask the children about their egg. They can

---

[17] From "The Strength of Goodness - School Aged Activity," by Jeannie Vogel, (https://www.focusonthefamily.com/parenting/the-strength-of-gentleness/). Reprinted with permission. Permission granted by author on March 10, 2025.

carry it in their hands, a shirt or pocket, or in another way, but they must not set the egg down, except to go to the bathroom.

Let life go on as usual. Don't remind anyone about his or her egg. As the children carry the eggs, at first, they will probably be careful, but they may eventually forget about their eggs and get careless. Even if the eggs do not crack, your children will find it difficult to be mindful of their eggs for the entire time.

Afterward, check on the eggs. Explain that these fragile eggs are like people's feelings. Sometimes we can accidentally say something that hurts a sibling or cousin's feelings. Or we can be reckless with our words and crush others. Gentleness means treating each person with care, similar to how we needed to care for the eggs. Explain that when we get busy with everyday life, we may find it hard to be careful with our words all the time. But we can ask God to help us be gentle and mindful of others.

Craft/Activity: Paper Plate Face Puppets

Supplies:

- Paper plates
- Markers or crayons
- Tape or stapler
- Craft sticks, popsicle sticks, or paint stirrers (4 per child)

Instructions:

1. Start by cutting each paper plate in half. Give each child at least four halves of paper plates.
2. On each half, draw different facial expressions, such as happy, sad, angry, or silly. Have them drawn from the nose down only.
3. Attach a craft stick, popsicle stick, or paint stirrer to each plate half using tape or a stapler, creating a puppet-like handle.

4. Let the children take turns holding up their puppets for the others to see. You can also have them look in a mirror to observe the different expressions they've created.
5. Keep the puppets available throughout the day to remind children of their emotions—happy, sad, angry, or silly—and encourage them to make good choices.

Gentleness: Day Three

Bible Story: Psalm 23—The Lord is My Shepherd

Read Psalm 23, or from *The Beginners Bible*, and Hebrews 12:1-11

Discussion Questions:

1. How is the shepherd gentle with his sheep?
   The shepherd feeds, guides, looks after, and provides everything the sheep need.
2. Do you think being quiet is like being gentle?
   What did David describe as a quiet place?
   David mentioned laying down on grass beside a peaceful stream as a quiet place.
3. How does God/Jesus show His gentleness when we are in a dark, scary place?
   God is with us, so we don't have to be afraid, even in scary times.
4. Do you think the shepherd ever had to discipline his sheep or protect them?
   Yes, sometimes the shepherd needs to protect or guide the sheep to keep them safe.
5. Do your parents ever discipline you?
   Consider the ways your parents guide you for your own good, even when it's not fun.

6. What kind of things do your parents ask you to do that are "good for you," but you may not always enjoy? Reflect on tasks like homework, chores, brushing your teeth, going to bed, or other activities that might not always be enjoyable but help you grow.
7. Does God/Jesus look after you like a shepherd?
   Think about how God guides and cares for you, just like a shepherd with his sheep.
8. Who is the Good Shepherd mentioned in the Bible? Where is He leading us?
   The Good Shepherd is Jesus, and He is leading us back to the heart of God and to have a relationship with God.
9. Is God/Jesus gentle with sinners?

   Yes, God and Jesus show gentleness to those who make mistakes, offering forgiveness and love.

Craft: Shepherd Hook/Staff

Oriental Trading[18] offer a really cute Psalm 23 staff that you can purchase, or if you are more creative than me, you can make your own.

Craft: Handprint Sheep

Supplies:

- Large piece of white cardstock
- Small piece of black or tan cardstock
- Glue
- Scissors
- Pencil
- 2 wiggly eyes
- 1 pink pom-pom – for nose
- Cotton balls

---

[18] https://www.orientaltrading.com/psalm-23-shepherd-s-staff-craft-kit-makes-12-a2-13585218.fltr

- Black marker
- White crayon

Instructions:

1. **Trace & Cut:**
   Using a pencil, trace the child's hand on the white cardstock, and carefully cut it out. Be sure the thumb is pointing out as that will be the face.
2. **Make the Legs:**
   Use the black marker to color the bottom of each finger—these will become the sheep's legs.
3. **Add Wool:**
   Glue cotton balls all over the palm area of the handprint to create the sheep's wool. Let it dry.
4. **Create the Face:**
   a. Cut an oval from the black cardstock for the sheep's head.
   b. Glue the wiggly eyes in the center of the oval.
   c. Attach the pink pom-pom underneath the eyes as the nose.
   d. Cut two small ears from the black cardstock and glue them to the top sides of the head.
   e. Glue the completed head over the thumb area of the handprint to represent the sheep's face. Let everything dry.
5. **Add Scripture:**
   Using a white crayon, write "Psalm 23" on the sheep's legs (child's fingers).
6. **Display Your Sheep:**
   Attach a magnet or ribbon to the back so the sheep can be hung on the fridge or in the child's room as a sweet reminder of God's care.

Craft: Sock Puppet Sheep

Supplies:

- White or black knee sock (or tube sock)
- Cardboard
- Yarn or cotton balls (for the sheep's wool)
- Red felt
- Pink felt
- White felt
- Googly eyes
- Hot glue gun (or tacky glue for younger children)
- Markers
- Crayons

Instructions:

1. **Prepare the Mouth:**
    a. Cut a piece of cardboard into a large oval, roughly the width of the child's hand. This will be used for the puppet's mouth.
    b. Fold the oval in half.
    c. Turn the sock inside out and lay it flat. Position the folded cardboard so that half is under the toe of the sock and the other half is on top, with the fold at the very end of the sock's toe.
    d. Use a hot glue gun to secure the cardboard in place. Let it dry completely. Once dry, turn the sock right side out.
2. **Position the Features:**
    a. Put your hand into the sock to mark where you want to place the eyes, nose, and ears. Use a marker to make small dots to guide you.
    b. Take your hand out of the sock and glue the googly eyes where you marked.

3. **Create the Mouth:**
    a. Cut a large oval from red or pink felt to fit over the mouth area, covering both the top and bottom of the cardboard.
    b. Insert the felt into the mouth area and use hot glue to secure it in place.
4. **Add the Tongue:**
    a. Cut a smaller piece of pink or red felt for the tongue.
    b. Glue the tongue into the back of the mouth.
5. **Make the Ears:**
    a. Cut out ear shapes from pink and white felt. The pink pieces should be smaller to mimic the inside of the ear.
    b. Glue the pink pieces onto the white pieces, then attach the finished ears to the sides of the sock's head, just above the eyes.
6. **Add the Wool:**
    a. Glue yarn or cotton balls onto the top of the sock for the sheep's wool. You can also cover the entire sock with wool if you like.
7. **Create the Nose:**
    a. Cut a small triangle from pink felt and glue it to the front of the face, just below the eyes, to form the sheep's nose.

The sock puppet sheep is now complete and ready for play! For younger children, use tacky glue instead of a hot glue gun to ensure safety. Have the children use their new sheep puppet to say their memory verse.

Snack

Choose another snack that you must be gentle with, like peaches, plums, nectarines, or berries. Ask the children "What happens if you drop one of these?" They can get bruised and turn brown. You must be gentle with them before you eat them.

Activity: Lie down in green pastures

Take a moment to step outside, lie down on the grass or a blanket, and simply be still. Listen to the sounds around you; this is like resting in green pastures and beside quiet waters. Stay there for as long as the children are able, soaking in the peace and serenity—the gentleness of the moment.

Activity: Being Gentle

Use this activity to help illustrate the effectiveness of gentleness. [19]

Supplies:

- Balloons
- Dish soap
- (Very) sharp bamboo skewer

You may want to practice this a time or two before trying in front of the children.

Use your fingers to lightly coat the skewer in dish soap. Then blow up a balloon, not inflating it too much. You should be able to dent the side of it with your finger. Now ask if your grandkids think it's possible to put the skewer through the balloon without popping it. They'll likely say, "No way."

Tell your grandkids that, with a gentle approach, it's possible to keep the balloon intact. Starting at the balloon's top (where the color is darkest), slowly spin the skewer as you gently push on the balloon. Keep spinning and gently pressing until the skewer goes into the balloon. Carefully push the skewer to the opposite side, next to the knot. Spin the skewer again, gently pushing it through to the outside of the balloon.

---

[19] From "The Strength of Goodness - Tween Activity," by Vance Fry, (https://www.focusonthefamily.com/parenting/the-strength-of-gentleness/). Reprinted with permission. Permission granted by author on March 15, 2025.

If the balloon pops, try again. When successful, let your grandkids skewer a balloon too, if you feel they are old enough to try. The younger ones probably won't want to try due to the fear that the balloon may pop.

Discussion Questions:

1. How were you able to skewer a balloon without it popping?
2. What would have happened if you used all your strength to force the skewer through? Explain that gentleness is sometimes more effective than sheer strength. This is especially true in our relationships. By using a gentle approach with others, we can talk more easily about difficult things with people. Read Philippians 4:5.
3. How can you show gentleness to your siblings? Your cousins?
4. If you had to speak a difficult truth to a friend, what approach would best preserve your friendship?

Gentleness: Day Four

Bible Lesson: Gentle words

Introduction - How Are We to Be Gentle With Our Words?

If children are old enough, assign each a verse to read:

- **Proverbs 15:1** (NASB) – "*A gentle answer turns away wrath, but a harsh word stirs up anger.*"
- **Proverbs 16:24** (NASB) – "*Pleasant words are a honeycomb, sweet to the soul and healing to the bones.*"
- **Proverbs 12:18** (NASB) – "*There is one who speaks rashly like the thrusts of a sword, but the tongue of the wise brings healing.*"
- **Colossians 4:6** (NIV) – "*Let your conversation always be full of grace, seasoned with salt, so that you may know how to answer everyone.*"

Discussion Questions:

1. Can you recall an instance when someone spoke harshly to you? How did it affect you?
2. When someone speaks unkindly or harshly to you, what emotions do you experience?
3. Why do you think pleasant words are like honeycomb? In Bible times, it was a prized commodity that was used for healing, nourishment, and satisfaction. Our words can be like this when they are pleasant.
4. According to the Bible, how should you respond when someone speaks to you angrily?
5. What are "reckless words" or speaking rashly? How does it feel when someone speaks that way to you?
6. How do pleasant and kind words make you feel?

Craft: Tie-Dye Shirts

Supplies:

- One white shirt per child (available at Michaels for an affordable price)
- Tie-dye kit (available at Michaels, Oriental Trading, or other craft stores)
- Plastic tablecloth to protect your work area

Instructions:

1. Distribute one white shirt to each child.
2. Follow the instructions in the tie-dye kit carefully.
3. Remind the children to be gentle and not to overuse any one color to avoid making the shirt too dark.
4. After they've finished dyeing their shirts, hang them up to dry.

5. Once the shirts are dry, allow the children to wear them home. This is a perfect photo opportunity to capture the moment with all the kids wearing their "camp" shirts!

Activity: Toothpaste Experiment

If you didn't complete this activity during the lesson on kindness (instructions on page 135), it aligns perfectly with today's lesson on gentleness and using gentle words. If you did the activity, ask the children if they remember it and discuss how, just like it's impossible to put toothpaste back into the tube, it's difficult to take back words once they've been spoken.

Activity: Crumpled picture

Start by drawing a picture of a person or cutting one out from a magazine. Then, crumple the paper into a very tight ball. Once it's tightly balled up, slowly open it back up and try to smooth it out flat. Work hard to remove all the wrinkles. Ask yourself, "Am I able to get it completely smooth again?"

Notice how the wrinkles in the paper are difficult to fully smooth out, no matter how hard you try. This is like mean words—they can't be taken back and leave a lasting impact, just like the creases in the paper. Remember to be gentle with your words and actions. They have the power to hurt or to show gentleness.

Activity: Visit to a Petting Zoo or Farm

Take the children to a petting zoo or farm where they can interact with animals. Before they approach the animals, explain that the animals need to be treated gently.

Discuss how animals can become frightened or upset if people are loud, aggressive, or rough with them. Ask the children, "Do you think the animals are more relaxed when they are handled gently?"

Encourage them to observe how the animals respond to soft, kind touches. Then ask, "What happens if the animals are not handled gently, like if they were hit or treated roughly?" Use this opportunity to reinforce the idea that, just like animals, people also need to be treated gently, with care and respect in order to feel safe and comfortable.

Snack

- Melons
- Ripe avocado

Activity: Soft Fuzzies vs. Hard Scratches

Take your grandchildren on a nature walk and help them find items that represent "soft fuzzies" or "hard scratches." The goal is to explore the difference between gentle and harsh things in nature, and how they relate to our words and actions.

Explain that soft fuzzies are items that are delicate and gentle, things that a light breeze could move or that are soft to the touch, such as dandelion fluff, moss, small seeds, leaves, and feathers. Ask the children to collect examples of these and place them in a zip-lock bag marked “soft fuzzies.”

Next, explain that hard scratches are items that are sturdy and unmovable even by a strong wind, or that might hurt if touched too roughly, such as sticks or small rocks. Let the children collect these and place them in a separate zip-lock bag marked “hard scratches.”

After the walk, return to a blanket outside and have the children take turns picking one item from each bag to share. Ask them to explain whether their item reminds them of something gentle and kind (like soft fuzzies) or something harsh and hurtful (like hard scratches), and why they feel that way.

Wrap-Up: Remind the children that when we are gentle with our words and actions, people enjoy being around us, and we are less likely to hurt others—physically or with unkind words.

Finally, end the activity by having the children recite their verses. Put on their tie-dyed shirts, and, if possible, record them saying their verse individually or as a group. This will be a great way to capture their learning and memories from the camp!

Display all the collected items as a reminder of gentleness.

Self-Control

Introduction

We are looking forward to hosting Grandkids Camp and teaching this year's theme through athletics. Eight grandchildren, ranging in age from 2 to 11, will be attending. I have a feeling we'll need plenty of self-control! One of our grandchildren, already aware that we're focusing on the Fruits of the Spirit, was quick to point out who he thought would benefit most from this particular fruit—and it wasn't himself, but rather a younger cousin. I gently reminded him that all of us need self-control at times.

Athletic Theme for Self-control

Memory Verse: 1 Corinthians 9:25

"*Every athlete exercises self-control in all things. They do it to receive a perishable wreath, but we an imperishable.*"

As you practice self-control, you will get stronger, much like an athlete who builds strength through regular training. Self-control requires you to stop and think before acting, answering, or doing something you might later regret.

Song – "Give Me Self-Control" by Sovereign Grace. This is such a fun song you can find on YouTube that can be played while they are working on crafts, eating meals, or anytime throughout the day. As you listen to the song for the first time, pause and make sure they understand the words, especially that they cannot have self-control without the help of Jesus, so we can be more like Him by practicing this. The Holy Spirit is the one who can fill us with this fruit of self- control. Chores are an excellent way to teach self-control. Assign age-appropriate tasks to each child, and if these chores need to be completed before moving on to other activities, make sure they understand the timing. This helps the children develop the self-control to finish their task before enjoying the next fun activity. Over the years, we've added various chores, like setting the table for meals, clearing the table afterward, and cleaning up toys. As they grow, the children can take on more responsibilities, such as loading and unloading the dishwasher, helping to prepare meals, filling water bottles, wiping down bathroom sinks, and more.

When you have many grandchildren, it's important for them to learn how to help with cleaning and other tasks so the responsibility doesn't fall solely on the grandparents. It's best to start them young when they find it fun to pitch in, building skills they can carry into adulthood.

Books on Self-control:

- *Howard B. Wigglebottom Learns to Listen* by Howard Binkow
- *Overdoing It* by Joy Berry
- *The Trouble with Larry* by Doug Peterson
- *Miss Nelson is Missing* by Harry G. Allard
- *The King who found his Self-Control* by Cosi & Christyn Hin

Self-Control: Day One

Self-control is the ability to manage your thoughts, emotions, and actions. It involves resisting immediate temptations and avoiding impulsive reactions in order to focus on more important goals, like learning, being kind, or achieving long-term success.

Discuss the memory verse with the grandchildren; it's important to help them fully understand its meaning by reading 1 Corinthians 9:24-27 for context. This passage compares the Christian life to a race, where self-control is key to reaching the goal.

Discussion Questions:

1. How does an athlete exercise self-control? Athletes must train hard, follow a strict routine, and resist temptations in order to stay focused on their goal.
2. What are "all things"? This refers to everything in life, meaning we should apply self-control in every area of our lives, not just in one part.
3. What does "perishable" mean? "Perishable" refers to things that don't last, like a wreath given to an athlete, which fades and decays over time.
4. What do athletes receive today instead of a wreath? Today, athletes may receive medals or trophies, but these are also temporary and will not last forever.
5. What does "imperishable" mean? "Imperishable" refers to things that last forever, like eternal life. This is what Christians (followers of Jesus) are striving for—something that doesn't fade away.

Help them see that just as an athlete works hard for a temporary prize, we are called to exercise self-control to win a much greater, eternal reward—eternal life with God.

Bible Story: 1 Samuel 24—David and Saul

David had been on the run for some time, hiding from King Saul, who was determined to capture and kill him; this was because Saul felt threatened by David's growing popularity and success. One day, someone informed Saul of David's whereabouts, and Saul set out to find him. This is where the story begins.

Read 1 Samuel 24

Discussion Questions:

1. What was Saul doing in the cave?

Saul was in the cave to rest. He had been pursuing David, who was hiding from him, and while on this pursuit, Saul unknowingly entered the very cave where David and his men were hiding. Saul went into the cave to relieve himself, which is why he was vulnerable and unaware of David's presence in the same location.

2. How did David show self-control?

David showed tremendous self-control in this situation. When his men urged him to take advantage of the opportunity to kill Saul, David resisted the temptation to harm the king. Instead, David chose to cut off a piece of Saul's robe, not take Saul's life. His restraint demonstrated his deep respect for Saul as the Lord's anointed king. Despite having the chance to end his years of fleeing and escape the threat of death, David trusted God's timing and refused to take matters into his own hands. He showed patience, honor, and faith in God's plan, refusing to take revenge.

3. Do you think you could have self-control if you knew someone was wanting to hurt you, and you had the opportunity to stop them?

This is a challenging question. It's natural for people to feel angry, afraid, or even vengeful when someone threatens or harms them. It would be difficult to show the same level of self-control as David in such a situation.

However, David's example teaches us the importance of trusting God, showing compassion, and not letting fear or anger control our actions. In situations like this, seeking God's wisdom and strength can help us respond in a way that reflects His values, even when faced with danger. It might be hard to imagine having such self-control, but with God's help, it's possible to act with grace and patience rather than revenge.

This story reminds us of the power of self-control and the importance of letting God guide our actions, even in the most difficult circumstances.

Activity: Make a cave (David and Saul)

This activity brings the story of David and Saul to life, allowing children to engage in a hands-on way to explore the themes of bravery and self-control.

Supplies:

- 1-2 large blankets
- 2-4 kitchen or dining room chairs
- A small piece of fabric (about 6"x6")
- Painter's tape

My kids always enjoyed the simple fun of putting a blanket over chairs and making a tent.

Instructions:

1. **Create the Cave:**
    a. Set up the "cave" by draping the blankets over 2-3 chairs, making sure it's large enough for someone to hide in the back (just like David did in the story).
    b. Make the space cozy and dark inside the cave, so the children can feel what it might have been like for David to hide from Saul.
2. **Assign Roles:**

   a. One child will be David, and the other will be Saul. If there are more children, you can rotate roles.
   b. **Saul:** Tape a small piece of cloth (the "robe" piece David cut off in the story) to the clothing of the child playing Saul. Saul will "sit" in the cave.
   c. **David:** The child playing David will try to sneak into the cave to grab the piece of cloth from Saul without being noticed.

3. **Time to Play:**
   a. Set a timer for each round (e.g., 1 minute) and let David try to get the piece of cloth from Saul while he is "sitting" in the cave.
   b. Make sure Saul remains seated or unaware of David's attempts (this mimics Saul being unaware in the story).
4. **Discuss the Experience:**
   a. After each round, talk with the children about their experiences.
5. **Discussion Questions:**
   a. How easy or difficult was it to get the piece of cloth?
   b. Did you feel scared when trying to grab the cloth? Why or why not?
   c. Do you think David was scared when he had the chance to harm Saul? Why or why not?

Activity: Play Hide-and-Seek with a Twist (David and Saul)

This game takes the classic hide-and-seek to a new level by incorporating the idea of David hiding from Saul. It also builds in elements of self-control and strategy—skills athletes use when planning how to win a game. If you have multiple children, you can have more than one "David" and/or more than one "Saul."

Instructions:

1. **Set Up the Game:**

   a. Choose an area where the children can hide behind furniture (like a door, under a bed, or behind a couch). The goal is for the children to hide in a place where they can see the person "looking" for them, but the seeker cannot see them.
   b. Decide who will be "David" (the person hiding) and who will be "Saul" (the person seeking). You can switch roles throughout the game.

2. **How to Play:**
   a. **David (the hider):** David must hide creatively in a spot where he can see Saul, but Saul cannot see him. David needs to wait until Saul gets close, but before Saul can find him, **David must try to touch Saul**.
   b. **Saul (the seeker):** Saul must walk around the room, trying to find David. Saul cannot see David, but he will hear or feel David's movements, so he must be alert.
3. **The Twist:**
   a. **David's Challenge:** Before Saul finds David, **David must touch Saul** without being detected. This adds an element of strategy and excitement to the game, just as David had to carefully and silently approach Saul in the cave.
   b. If David touches Saul before Saul finds him, the game continues. If Saul finds David first, the round ends, and they can switch roles.

Discussion Points:

1. Did you come up with a strategy as an athlete would in order to win at their sport?
2. Was it hard to get close to the seeker without being noticed?
3. Did you feel scared when you were hiding, or did you feel confident?

4. How did it feel when you were able to touch the person without being seen, just like David had to avoid being noticed by Saul?
5. Do you think David felt fear when he was hiding from Saul? How did he stay calm and make the right choice?
6. As David, did you feel you had to have self-control to make sure you touched Saul without him noticing?

Activity: Think it or say it

Come up with a list of things that kids typically might say in life and in sport and help them decide which statements are appropriate and which ones they should keep to themselves. This is a great way to practice self-control.

For example (using things you might hear from your grandchildren or items related to athletes):

- "Your clothes look funny."
- “I am the best athlete”
- “You are very good at running”
- "You have a big nose."
- "This is so much fun!"
- "I don't want to play with you."
- "I always win."
- "I'm better than you."
- "You did a great job!"
- "I like your picture/craft."
- "Me first!"
- “He/She always gets to go first”
- “I want…”

Snack: Peanut Butter Bread

Tell the children that David ate bread that had been offered to God while he was running from King Saul. Just like David needed strength, athletes today need protein to help build strong muscles. Peanut butter is a great source of protein. Another fun option could be peanut butter crackers!

Craft: Spear

Supplies:

- Card stock or construction paper (one piece per child)
- A piece of cloth or an old rag to cut up
- 1 straw or pipe cleaner per child
- Aluminum foil

Instructions:

1. Have the children create a spear using the straw or pipe cleaner.
2. Help them fold a triangle from the aluminum foil to make the tip of the spear.
3. Glue the spear and the foil tip to the paper.
4. Cut a small piece of fabric from the rag or cloth and have the children glue it onto the paper as well.
5. Ask the children to write (or write for them) the phrase: "David had self-control and spared Saul's life. 1 Samuel 24."

This craft helps the children reflect on David's act of self-control when he spared Saul's life.

Activity: Whittle a Stick into a Spear

Supplies:

- Small Stick found outside
- Pocket Knife
- Large Rock
- Fabric or Paper Napkins

Instructions:

1. Teach the older kids how to safely whittle a point on a stick to create their own spear. Make sure they understand proper whittling techniques and safety precautions.
2. Younger children can shape the end of a stick by rubbing it against a rough rock until it gradually forms a point.
3. Once the spear is sharp enough, challenge them to see if they can pierce a piece of fabric or a paper napkin and pick it up.
4. Remind them to be careful and not to spear their siblings or cousins during this activity. Emphasize safety at all times.
5. For some outdoor fun, they can take their spears outside and try to spear leaves or other items found in nature. Remind them that spears should never be used toward animals or people, including siblings and cousins. Later, let them use their spears for roasting marshmallows over a campfire and enjoy making s'mores together!

This activity combines skill-building and patience, which are both required by athletes, while allowing the kids to connect with the story of David in a hands-on way.

Self-Control: Day Two

Bible Story: Nehemiah 4—Nehemiah returned to Jerusalem

Discussion Questions:

1. How did Nehemiah show self-control?
   Nehemiah showed self-control by not fighting back when others opposed him.
2. Why did he not fight back and instead exercise self-control?
   Nehemiah knew that God would protect them, so he trusted in God's plan rather than resorting to violence.

3. What did he do instead of fighting back?
   Nehemiah stationed guards to protect the workers while they rebuilt the walls.
4. When are times you need to exercise self-control? When someone takes a toy you're playing with? When you lose a game? When someone calls you a name, hurts your feelings or laughs at you? When you're an athlete and you don't win a game or race?

This is also a good opportunity to talk about times when your grandchildren may struggle with self-control and help them think about how to handle those situations with patience and trust in God.

Activity: Relay Race with Self-Control

Instructions:

1. Organize a relay race where children have to exercise self-control by waiting for their teammate to reach them before they can take off.
2. The race can be a simple running relay, or you can get creative and add fun challenges based on the children's ages. For example, they could hop on one foot, balance an object on their head, or complete a small obstacle course before handing off the baton (or another item) to their teammate.
3. Emphasize the importance of patience and self-control while waiting for their turn to run. This helps teach them how to be calm and focused while they wait for the next part of the race.

This activity not only encourages physical exercise but also helps children practice self-control in a fun and engaging way.

Snack: Dried Fruit or Trail Mix

This snack is something an athlete or a hiker might carry because it's easy to transport and provides energy, which helps in building self-control. Just like the people of Jerusalem, who may not have had fresh fruits and vegetables, they could have had dried fruits as practical and nutritious options.

Dried fruit or trail mix makes for a healthy snack throughout the week. It's a great alternative to crackers or candy and can give you a boost of energy when needed!

Snack/Craft: Build a House

Supplies:

- Mini and/or full-size marshmallows
- Graham crackers
- Frosting
- Paper plates
- Gumdrops or similar type candy

Instructions:

1. Give each child a paper plate.
2. Using the graham crackers, have the children build a house in the middle of the paper plate. If needed, they can use frosting to help hold the pieces together. (They'll probably say they need it!)
3. Once the house is built, encourage the children to create a wall around it to protect it. This is where they will need to exercise self-control as they carefully build their wall using marshmallows and frosting to "protect" their house. They can decide how high they want the wall to be for protection.
4. After the walls are built, they can take turns throwing gumdrops across the table to try and knock down each other's houses. Set a time frame for the throwing challenge.
5. During the game, remind them to practice self-control and not get upset if their house falls down. It's all part of the fun!
6. Once the time is up, they can either save their project or enjoy eating their creation.

This activity combines creativity, fun, and a chance to practice self-control in a playful way!

Activity: Jenga

Playing Jenga requires self-control, as it challenges players to make thoughtful decisions and take their time with each move. Similarly, talk about how a wall can collapse if it's not constructed properly or if there are gaps in its structure. Just like a city's defenses would be weakened by holes in a wall, a Jenga tower becomes unstable when pieces are removed carelessly. If not built solidly, a wall or the Jenga tower will eventually fall.

Activity: Build a wall

Supplies:

- Blocks, Dominos or similar type items
- Bean bags or small soft balls

To bring the story to life, have the children build a wall. Assign one or more children as guards and designate one or two others as enemies attempting to knock the wall down using a bean bag or small soft ball. The guards' job is to protect the wall and prevent it from falling. Set a time limit for both building the wall and trying to knock it down. Afterward, allow the children to switch roles so everyone gets a chance to play different parts.

Craft: Glitter Jar

Supplies:

- One clear glass jar for each child (preferably smaller than 1 quart size)
- Glue - large bottle
- Various sizes and colors of glitter

- Printout of the words "Exercise self-control in all things" to fit on each lid

Instructions:

1. Pour water into the jar, then add a generous squeeze of glue. The glue helps the glitter swirl around inside the jar.
2. Let the children choose the colors and shapes of glitter to add to their jar.
3. Seal the jar tightly with the lid and shake gently to watch the glitter swirl.
4. Explain that when we don't exercise self-control, our thoughts and emotions can get all stirred up, just like the glitter inside the jar. It becomes hard to focus, stay calm, and exercise self-control.
5. Whenever the children feel like they are losing self-control, they can shake their jars, repeat the part of the verse, and pray for help to "exercise self-control in all things," while watching the glitter slowly settle down.

This activity helps remind children how self-control works—when we stay calm and focused, our thoughts and emotions settle, just like the glitter in the jar.

Self-Control: Day Three

Bible Story: Matthew 4:1-11—Jesus in the Wilderness[20]

In this story, Jesus demonstrates great self-control, resisting temptation in every way we might be tempted. Before reading the story ask the children: Have you ever skipped a meal? Or gone a whole day without food? Jesus

---

[20]Adapted From "Self-Control Bible Lesson (Fruit of the Spirt)," by Kara Jenkins, Ministry-to-Children by Tony Kumer, (https://ministry-to-children.com/self-control-bible-lesson-fruit-of-the-spirit/) - Copyright © 2025 **Creative Commons Attribution-ShareAlike 4.0 International**.

went without food for forty days. How do you think He felt? Was He hungry, tired, dizzy, or weak?
Explain that Satan tried to get Jesus to sin, tempting Him when He was at His weakest. Satan also tempts us when we are weak. Ask the children to listen for the different temptations Satan presents to Jesus. When they hear a temptation, have them put their hands on top of their heads.

Read Matthew 4:1-11

Discussion Questions:

1. Matthew 4:1-3 (children should place their hands on their heads). What does Satan ask Jesus to do?
2. Matthew 4:4-6 (hands on heads). What does Satan ask Jesus to do?
3. Matthew 4:7-9 (hands on heads). What does Satan ask Jesus to do?

   Give Jesus a round of applause for showing self-control, even when He was weak, tired, and hungry!
4. What did Jesus keep saying to Satan? *"It is written."* Explain that Jesus used Scripture to fight against Satan. He knew the Word of God, and there is no better weapon for resisting temptation. The Word of God helps us develop self-control!

Application:

Is there an area in your life where you need self-control? Is it your tongue? Do you gossip or complain? Do you use language that would hurt the heart of God? Or perhaps it's in your actions —do you struggle to control your hands or yourself when you're angry or frustrated about something? Do you hit, push, or kick? What about your free time? Do you spend time with God each day? Do you help around the house and keep up with your schoolwork, or do you lack self-control and spend too much time on the computer, watching TV, or playing video games? With the help of Jesus living inside of us, we can have self-control by the power of His Holy Spirit.

Snack: Homemade Bread

You can involve the kids in making the bread from scratch if you'd like, or for an easier option, you can buy frozen bread loaves. If you're using frozen loaves, let them sit out to thaw first thing in the morning, or you can put them in the refrigerator the night before.

Once thawed, place the loaves on a greased sheet pan or greased loaf pan, then cover them with a towel. They will need a good part of the day to rise. This process takes self-control as the children wait for the bread to rise. When the dough has risen past the top of the loaf pan, bake it according to the package instructions.

After baking, remove the bread from the oven and allow the kids to enjoy a slice with butter and/or honey.

Ask, "Do you think you could live on just this bread?"

Activity: Minute to Win It Candy Game

As athletes exercise self-control and practice to improve their skills, these challenges will require the same. You may not succeed the first time, but always do your best.

Supplies:

- Quart-sized container for each child to collect their candy prizes
- Various types of candy: M&M's, Skittles, fruit snacks, candy corn, gumdrops, or any candy that can stand up, plus flat candies or cereal like Life Savers or Fruit Loops or Cheerios that can be stacked
- Chopsticks (one for each child)
- Bowls
- Plastic spoons

- Plates
- Marshmallows

Instructions:

Tell the children they must practice self-control and not eat any candy until the game is over.

Candy on the Spoon Race:

1. Fill a bowl with small candies like M&M's, Skittles, or fruit snacks.
2. Tape a start line and place one cup for each child about five feet away (adjust the distance based on age—older children go farther maybe one foot per year).
3. Give each child a plastic spoon.
4. Explain they will have one minute to move as many candies as possible from the bowl to their cup using only the spoon.
5. If the candy falls off the spoon, they must return to the start line.
6. Use a timer on your phone and make sure it's loud enough for the children to hear.
7. When the timer goes off, they must stop. The child with the most candies in their cup wins and can place them in their bag.

Stand Up the Candy:

1. Give each child a plate.
2. Tell them they have one minute to stand up as many pieces of candy corn (or any candy that stands up such as gum drops) as possible.
3. The child with the most candy standing when the timer goes off can put it in their treat bag.

Candy Stacking:

1. Provide a bowl of flat candies (like Life Savers) or cereal (Fruit Loops, Cheerios).

2. On a plate, they will have one minute to stack as many candies or cereal pieces as possible.
3. When the timer goes off, the child with the tallest stack wins and gets to add the candy to their bag.

Chopstick Pickup:

1. Place a bowl of Fruit Loops near each child, along with a plate and a pair of chopsticks.
2. The children must use the chopsticks to transfer the Fruit Loops from the bowl to their plate.
3. Whoever has the most Fruit Loops on their plate when the timer goes off wins the Fruit Loops.
4. Remind them they can't use their hands. Some may figure out they can pick up multiple loops at once, which will be fun to watch!

Marshmallow Toss:

1. Have each child return to the start line used for the spoon race.
2. Place a small bowl of marshmallows near each child and place another bowl about five feet away (or adjust the distance based on age).
3. When the timer starts, the children must try to toss as many marshmallows into their bowl as possible within one minute.
4. They can toss one at a time or several at once.
5. When the timer goes off, the person with the most marshmallows in their bowl wins them.

After the Game:
Once the game is over, award prizes to all participants, especially those who didn't win one of the rounds. You could also have a first and second-place winner for each task. Remind the children to practice self-control, be good sports, and not complain about how much or how little someone else has. This is a great opportunity for the winners to share their winnings.

Craft: Tissue Paper Cross Craft

Supplies:

- Cardboard or cardstock cut into the shape of a cross
- Tissue paper cut into small 1-inch squares
- Glue
- Magnet or string

Instructions:

1. Give each child a cross and some colored tissue paper squares.
2. Instruct them to spread a thin layer of glue on their cross, working in sections if necessary.
3. Next, have them crinkle each tissue paper square by gathering the four corners together, then attach it to the cross. They should cover the entire surface, putting the tissue paper very close and arranging the tissue paper either in a pattern or randomly.
4. Once the cross is covered, glue a magnet to the back so it can be displayed on a refrigerator, or add a string for hanging it in their room.
5. Encourage the children to remember that whenever they face temptation and need self-control, they can look at the cross and know that Jesus was also tempted but though tempted, He did not sin, and, in fact, sacrificed His life for our sins.

Self- Control: Day Four

Bible Story: Judges 13:1-5, 13:24-14:4, 16:4-30—Samson

Introduction:

Samson's story is about a man with incredible strength—doesn't that sound like an athlete? He also had very long hair, which played a crucial role in his strength. Listen closely to learn why his hair was so important.

In this story, there are good guys and bad guys—can you figure out who they are?

Read Judges 13:1-5, 13:24-14:4

Discussion Questions:

1. What did God promise Samson?
   God promised to make Samson a great warrior. But Samson had to make promises to God.
2. Can you remember the three promises he made? He promised:
   a. Never to cut his hair.
   b. Not to touch anything unclean or dirty.
   c. Not to drink alcohol.
3. Did God keep His promise?
   Yes, He did. God made Samson incredibly strong—stronger than your dad or grandpa!
4. What did God want Samson to use his strength for?
   God wanted Samson to rescue the Israelites from the Philistines.
5. Did Samson keep his promises?
   No, unfortunately, Samson made a lot of bad choices.
6. Which promises did he break? He broke every one of the promises he made to God
7. Why do you think he broke those promises?
   Samson lacked self-control.
8. Do you remember what self-control is?
   Self-control is the ability to resist temptation and make the right choices, even when it's difficult. For example, when you lose a game or don't get as much candy as you hoped.

Samson was tempted by a beautiful woman and married her, even though it wasn't the best decision.

Read Judges 16:4-30

Discussion Questions:

1. Who were the good guys? The Israelites.
2. Who were the bad guys? The Philistines.

This story teaches us about self-control and keeping our promises, even when temptation is strong. Without self-control, we can end up in trouble.

Self-control takes practice, just like an athlete trains to get better. To become more like Jesus, we need to practice doing things that help us go God's way.

3. What are some things that can help you go God's way? Reading the Bible and obeying what it says. Praying for self-control. You also need to listen to the Holy Spirit, who will guide you in the right direction. With this kind of training, you'll make the right choices.

But remember, we're not perfect, and we all mess up sometimes. When we do, we need to confess our mistakes and try again. Just like athletes practice to get better, we can improve with practice too. We have God's help, just like He helped Samson once he humbled himself and asked for strength one last time.

4. How did God help Samson at the end of the story?
   At the end, Samson's strength was restored, and he was able to rescue the Israelites.

This reminds us that with God's help, we can overcome temptation and make the right choices!

Craft: Samson Paper Bag Puppet

Supplies:

- Brown paper bags (1 per child)
- Brown paper matching the color of the bags
- Brown or black yarn

- Crayons/Markers
- Wiggly eyes
- Scissors
- Glue

Instructions:

1. Start by cutting strong, muscular arms from the brown paper and gluing them to the sides of the bag, making it appear as if the puppet is flexing.
2. Draw clothes on the "body" section of the bag.
3. Next, draw a nose just above the fold of the bag and attach wiggly eyes.
4. For the hair, let the children choose the length, then cut strips of yarn that are twice as long and attach them in the middle at the top of the puppet's head. Use around five or more strips of yarn and glue or tape them in place.
5. Once finished, the children can use their puppets to act out or play through the story.

Activity: Strength under pressure

Supplies:

Empty soda cans

Many of us have tried balancing on an empty soda can before. If you haven't, let me show you how. Place one foot gently on top of the can while holding onto a chair or wall for support. Now it's your turn—go ahead and try to balance. Feel how strong the can is? It can hold your weight surprisingly well!

That strength reminds me of Samson. He was incredibly strong, just like this can. But sometimes, we make poor choices, just like he did. Do you remember what he did wrong? He chose to listen to someone else instead of obeying God. Because of that, God took away his strength.

Now, let's see what happens when we put a dent in the can. I'll dent it before or while you're balancing on it. What happens now? It collapses, right? That dent is like sin in our lives. When we let sin in, it weakens us and pulls us away from God—just like the dent weakens the can.

Can you stand on a dented can and expect it to hold you up? Of course not! And sin does the same to us. But here's the good news: When we confess our sins to God, He forgives us and removes those dents. He gives us strength again, just like He gave Samson strength one last time.

Now try balancing again—first on a dented can, then on one that's whole. Feel the difference?

Activity: Bubbles—What Happens When You Blow Bubbles?

Many children love to run, jump, and try to catch bubbles when they appear. To teach them self-control, have the children sit in a circle, with you as the grandparent sitting in the center. Begin blowing bubbles and tell the children that they must remain seated and use self-control. They are allowed to pop the bubbles that come to them. Afterward, let each child have a turn blowing bubbles, which requires a little less self-control. Ask them which was easier: sitting still and using self-control or blowing the bubbles? It's always fun to play, but it's not always easy to practice self-control, and sometimes it's important to remember that not all moments are for fun but to learn more.

After the lesson, let the children have fun blowing bubbles. You can either use the bubble recipe from Chapter 2 and the recipe section, or opt for pre-made bubbles

Activity: Board and Card Games

Almost any fun game you have at home can help your grandchildren practice self-control. To focus on the specific self-control skills involved in playing games, provide visual reminders that your grandchildren can refer to throughout the game. All board games, for example, require self-control as players must wait their turn to play.

Other games that help teach self-control include *Red Light, Green Light*; *Freeze Tag*, *Simon Says* (or "PaQ Says"/"Grandpa Says.") These games require your grandchildren to listen carefully and follow instructions, practicing control over their actions.

You can also play *Ready, Set, Go*, where you change the word "Go" to other instructions, such as "Stop" or "Hop," forcing the children to listen and show self-control before acting.

Activity: Role-Play Scenarios: Teaching Self-Control

1. **Scenario 1: Waiting for Turn in Line**
    a. **What happens without self-control:**
    The child impatiently pushes to the front of the line, shoves other children, or starts to complain loudly because they want to go first.
    b. **How to show self-control:**
    The child waits for their turn quietly, perhaps by counting in their head, keeping their hands to themselves, taking deep breaths, or praying for God to help them to wait patiently. You can model saying, “I can wait patiently with God’s help because I know everyone gets a turn.”
2. **Scenario 2: Sharing Toys**
    a. **What happens without self-control:**
    A child grabs a toy from another child, takes it without asking, or starts to cry because they don’t want to share.
    b. **How to show self-control:**
    The child asks politely, “Can I have a turn when you’re done?” or says, “I’ll wait until you’re finished, then it will be my turn.” They can also offer a different toy in exchange to practice sharing.
3. **Scenario 3: Managing Disappointment**

a. **What happens without self-control:**
   A child throws a tantrum or cries loudly when they don't get what they want (e.g., not getting the prize, losing a game).
b. **How to show self-control:**
   The child takes a deep breath and calmly says, "I'm disappointed, but that's okay. I'll try again next time." You can also model quoting a verse from the Bible or even the verse from this week "exercise self-control."

4. **Scenario 4: Interrupting While Someone is Talking**
   a. **What happens without self-control:**
      A child interrupts someone mid-sentence, loudly speaking over others because they're eager to share their thoughts.
   b. **How to show self-control:**
      The child waits for the other person to finish speaking, practicing patience. You can model saying, "I'll wait for my turn to talk," reinforcing that everyone deserves a chance to speak. Or teach them to say "excuse me," then wait till it is their turn.

In each of these role-play scenarios, you can demonstrate the behaviors you want to see and provide positive reinforcement when the child shows self-control.

Activity: Baking Soda and Vinegar Reaction – Learning About Self-Control

Supplies:

- Box of baking soda
- Bottle of vinegar
- Bowl or sink

Instructions:

1. Start by placing some baking soda into the bowl or sink.
2. Slowly pour vinegar onto the baking soda and watch the exciting fizzing and bubbling reaction.
3. Explain to the children: "When we lack self-control, it's like this reaction. We get all foamed up, and we might boil over, just like the vinegar and baking soda. But with self-control, we can stay calm instead of exploding."
4. Let the children try pouring the vinegar themselves, while guiding them to practice staying calm and controlled with their actions.

Reflection:

After the experiment, ask the children, "How did the baking soda and vinegar react when they came together? What can happen when we don't have self-control?" Talk about how the reaction was strong and quick, but with self-control, they can avoid overreacting and stay calm.

Activity: Fizzy Mess with shaken up Soda bottle- https://kidsofintegrity.com/activity/self-control/fizzy-mess/

Activity: Gum or Candy Self- Control

Supplies:

- Gum
- Candy
- Timer

Give each of the children either a piece of bubble gum or a small candy that they might want to chew and eat quickly but ask them to leave it on their tongue and not bite it. Set a time to see how long they have self-control. The last to bite it wins.

Activity: Giggle Game

This fun activity helps your grandkids practice self-control by challenging them not to laugh. Have them take turns sitting in a chair while the others try to make them laugh within thirty seconds. They can use any creative method they like—but make sure to remind them of the one important rule: no touching the person in the chair!

If the child sitting laughs, the one who made them laugh gets to switch places. During the game, remind everyone of their Bible verse to help connect the activity to the lesson on self-control.

You can even join in! Try what PaQ does—pretend to tickle under their arms without actually touching them. Say, "I'm not tickling or touching you!" and watch the giggles come. It's a fun way to help them practice keeping a straight face while learning to stay in control.

Craft: Stop Light

Supplies Needed:

- Black piece of paper
- Red, yellow, and green construction paper

Instructions:

Create a stoplight by gluing red, yellow, and green circles onto the black paper. Label each circle with "Stop," "Think," and "Act/Speak kind words." Print the Bible verse at the bottom of the page; this serves as a helpful reminder of how to practice self-control during tempting situations.

Reflections:

Self-control may not come easily—especially in a lively group of cousins—but that is precisely why it matters. By week's end, we hope that each of us, grandchildren and grandparents alike, will discover new ways to practice this Fruit of the Spirit both on and off the field. And with the help of the Holy Spirit, we can all learn to exercise self-control. May the truths planted through Scripture, activities, and creativity grow into lasting habits that help each child—and each of us—follow God with a steadier heart and a more self-controlled spirit.

My Notes:

My Notes

Conclusion

Working through each of these chapters has been a rewarding journey of learning. Many people have seen my social media posts and shared how they were taking notes from what we did at Grandkids Camp to use for their own camps. Now, all those notes are gathered in one place, ready for you to refer to whenever needed. While we held our Grandkids Camp over several days with our grandkids, you can easily pick a chapter, day, or activity to enjoy with your grandchildren whenever you see them, investing in their future with each moment spent together.

It's my hope that one day, my own children and grandchildren will use this book with their grandchildren, keeping the legacy going. It's a wonderful way to share the Bible and teach how to live it out daily.

Spending time with our grandchildren is something I treasure, as I'm sure you do. We love having fun together, but nothing fills my heart with more joy than hearing them quote verses and songs from Grandkids Camp. It reminds me of a verse I learned as a child, Psalm 119:11 (KJV): *"Thy word have I hid in mine heart, that I might not sin against thee."* They are now hiding God's Word in their hearts, just as I prayed they would. This is my prayer for them as we continue with Grandkids Camp each year, revisiting lessons with grandchildren who missed them and for future grandchildren.

This book is as much a tool for me as it is for everyone else. My prayer is that you are blessed as you work through each lesson, just as we were, learning and being convicted many times about our faith walk with God while teaching our grandchildren. Before I close, if you're not yet convinced about hosting a Grandkids Camp, I'd like to share some memories from my grandchildren and those who attended my parents' Grandkids Camp. I asked them to share some of their favorite or funniest moments.

The consensus on the funniest moment at our Grandkids Camp was when PaQ "slipped" on a banana peel. I'm pretty sure the kids still think he really fell. They were having bananas for a snack, and the youngest either dropped or tossed his peel onto the floor. PaQ walked over, then dramatically "slipped" on the peel and fell with his feet flying up in the air. They all laughed so hard in the moment—and they still crack up every time they remember it.

Our four-year-old grandson said his favorite activity was swimming. Our six-year-old granddaughter liked getting shaved ice, but she also enjoyed the activity from the lesson on talents—cutting corners—because the more corners we cut, the more corners there were. It helped her understand that we should share our talents with others.

Our seven-year-old granddaughter liked the craft where we made a fire (a small light-up one), and she used it as a night light in her room until the light stopped working. Our eight-year-old grandson had several favorites—collecting items in the woods and gluing them onto a plate, especially since his brother only collected rocks. He also liked the lesson on faithful friends, saying, "Jonathan was a faithful friend, and if you're going to be a friend, you should be faithful too." The oldest grandson enjoyed the craft where we painted over the word "Joy" on a canvas, then peeled off the letters to reveal the word underneath. He also liked the lesson on kindness because, as he put it, "When my cousin knocked my toy into the lake and we never found it, I needed to be kind."

At the top of the list from Poppop and Mammaw's Grandkids Camp (my parents' Grandkids Camp) was a memory from when they were camping in Pennsylvania. The girls stayed in the camper with Mammaw, and the youngest granddaughter rolled off the table bed, onto the floor, and out the door, continuing to sleep on the camper steps. Mammaw found her there the next morning, contently sleeping.

Another favorite memory was when Poppop and Mammaw took a smaller group of grandkids to Toccoa Falls College. It was just three—two girls and one boy. The girls came up with the idea of dressing the boy as a girl and walking around the campus, introducing themselves as Mr. Dave and Miss Anna's three youngest granddaughters. Word eventually got back to Poppop through one of his coworkers when he asked about his three granddaughters! They still talk and laugh about this story as adults.

The grandchildren all seemed to really enjoy doing crafts. Poppop found some wooden 3D dinosaur puzzles for each child to complete, and it was clear how much they loved them because they kept those puzzles for a long time (which I have yet to find for my own Grandkids Camp).

My daughter, who is the oldest of Poppop and Mammaw's grandchildren and the mother of the oldest of our grandchildren, put it perfectly:

"The thing that has stayed with me into adulthood is the fond memories of being with my cousins and grandparents. It's special that my parents are now sharing those same moments with their grandkids and cousins. Grandkids Camp means family is important. I once posted a quote on Facebook about cousins being your first friends, and that's really what Grandkids Camp was all about—being with your closest friends and special grandparents."

She continued with more thoughts:

"Grandkids Camp defines the essence of a happy childhood: carefree, happy, and surrounded by the people we love. Of course, as we've all gotten older, real life has brought its challenges—whether it's marriage or relationship issues, infertility, an unplanned pregnancy, mental health struggles, a desire to be married, or the pain of loss. But Grandkids Camp always reminds me of a time without worries or responsibility."

The joy they experienced at Grandkids Camp is re-lived every time they get together, even though Poppop and Mammaw will probably not be able to host another Grandkids Camp for their adult grandchildren. As you can see from these photos below, they truly love being together and recreating those fun memories.

1995 Pre-Grandkids Camp

2001 First year of Grandkids Camp

February 2024: They still love hanging out, and lovingly and respectfully left the open spot for one who has gone on to be with Jesus.

The investment you make in your grandchildren will echo through generations (as you see from these photos). As Psalm 145:4 says, "*One generation shall commend your works to another, and shall declare your mighty acts*." And in Psalm 71:17-18, "*O God, from my youth you have taught me, and I still proclaim your wondrous deeds. So even to old age and gray hairs, O God, do not forsake me, until I proclaim your might to another generation, your power to all those to come*."

As God allows me, even into old age (am I there yet?) and with a few gray hairs (I have a few!), I will continue hosting Grandkids Camp and proclaiming God's might to the next generation. My family may have a history of following Jesus, but even if yours doesn't, it can start with you and your grandchildren. May God use you to impact generations to come, and as Proverbs 17:6a says, *Grandchildren are the crown of the aged*, be motivated to wear your crown well.

My Notes:

My Notes:

Appendix A

Invitations

For those who wish to create invitations, Canva is a helpful and user-friendly resource. Here is a sample.

Love:

Goodness: I designed an invitation that fit snugly as a sleeve over a can. After printing and cutting it out, I gave one can/invitation to each family.

CAN we tempt you to come to

Grandkids Camp

Date:

Theme: Goodness

Place/Location:

Be prepared to show goodness by bringing two cans of your favorite item.

It could be soup, vegetables, tuna, or any favorite canned item.

MaQ and PaQ

Appendix A

Faithfulness:

Appendix B

Recipes

Homemade bubbles

- 6 cups distilled water
- 1-2 cup Joy dish soap
- 1-2 tablespoons glycerin

Dirt with Worms

Supplies:

- Clear plastic cups (1 per child): The clear cups allow you to see the layers
- 2 cups cold milk
- 1 package Oreos (crushed into crumbs)
- 1 package (4 oz) instant chocolate pudding
- 1 (8 oz) package Cool Whip
- Gummy worms

Instructions:

1. **Mix the Pudding**

   a. Pour the cold milk into a mixing bowl and add the instant pudding mix.
   b. Whisk together until well blended.
   c. Let the pudding sit for about 5 minutes to thicken.
2. **Combine with Cool Whip:**
   a. Gently fold the Cool Whip into the pudding until the mixture is uniform in color.
3. **Crush the Oreos:**
   a. Place Oreos in a large zip bag and crush them. This is a fun task for the kids
4. **Layer the Cup**
   a. Start by adding about 1 tablespoon of crushed Oreos to the bottom of each cup.
   b. Next, layer in the chocolate pudding.
   c. Repeat the layers of Oreos and pudding until the cups are filled.
5. **Hide the Worms:**
   a. For a fun surprise, place gummy worms in one of the layers instead of on top, so the kids have to dig to find them.
6. **Finish Off:**
   a. Top with a final layer of crushed Oreos.
   b. Chill in the refrigerator or enjoy immediately if the kids can't wait!

Homemade Playdoh

Supplies:

- 3 cups flour
- 3/4 cup table salt
- 4-5 tablespoons cream of tartar

- 3 cups water
- 3 tablespoons vegetable oil
- Food coloring
- Essential oils for a pleasant scent

Instructions:

1. Add the first five ingredients to a large pot and cook over medium heat, stirring continuously.
2. Gradually mix in food coloring, adding a few drops at a time until you achieve your desired hue. I added the color at the end to create different colors in smaller batches as I wanted various colors—just knead it in well. You might want to wear gloves to prevent staining your hands.
3. Continue stirring the mixture over heat until it begins to thicken. Use a silicone spatula to help pull the thickening dough away from the sides and bottom of the pot. Once the mixture forms a ball in the center, remove it from the heat.
4. Transfer the ball onto a lightly floured cutting board or cookie sheet. Carefully knead it until smooth. This is also the time to mix in more food coloring and essential oils, especially if you want to improve the smell of the playdough.
5. Once the playdough has cooled, store it in airtight containers or zip-lock bags to keep it fresh.
6. For construction-themed playdough, consider adding one or more of the following items to small batches:

- Sand
- Organic dirt
- Pea gravel
- Mulch
- Shells

Cream Wafer Recipe from Lynn Stieber:

Ingredients:

For the Filling (I sometimes double this because it's so delicious):

- ¼ cup soft butter
- ¾ cup sifted powdered sugar
- 1 egg yolk
- 1 teaspoon vanilla extract
- Food coloring (optional)

For the Cookies:

- 1 cup butter or margarine
- ⅓ cup whipping cream
- 2 cups flour
- Sugar (for coating)

Directions:

1. **Prepare the Cookie Dough**: In a bowl, mix the butter, whipping cream, and flour until thoroughly combined. Chill the dough for 1 hour.
2. **Preheat the Oven**: Set your oven to 375°F (190°C).
3. **Roll Out the Dough**: On a lightly floured surface, roll the dough to about 1/8 inch thick. Cut into 1½-inch rounds using a small biscuit cutter.
4. **Sugar Coating**: Transfer the cookie rounds to a bowl with sugar and coat both sides.
5. **Prepare for Baking**: Place the cookies on an ungreased baking sheet. Prick each cookie in 3-4 places with a fork.
6. **Bake**: Bake for 9-10 minutes or until the cookies are slightly puffy.
7. **Make the Filling**: In a bowl, blend the soft butter, powdered sugar, egg yolk, and vanilla until smooth. Tint with food coloring if desired.

8. **Assemble**: Once cooled, put two cookies together with the filling. This recipe makes about five dozen cookies.

Smoothie Recipe

Ingredients:

- 1 cup frozen blueberries or strawberries
- 1/2 cup vanilla (or plain) Greek yogurt
- 1 cup of your favorite milk
- 1 frozen banana (or use fresh ones from the lesson if you still have them)
- Optional: honey, to taste

Instructions:

Place all the ingredients into the blender and blend until smooth. Pour, enjoy, and savor the deliciousness!

Coin Craft Recipe

Supplies:

- 1 microwavable cup for each child
- 2 tablespoons baking soda
- 1 tablespoon cornstarch
- 1.5 tablespoons water
- Paints (for decoration)
- Optional: Biscuit cutters (for shaping)
- Modeling clay (as an alternative to the homemade recipe)

Instructions:

1. **For Homemade Clay**: Mix the baking soda, cornstarch, and water together in a bowl. Microwave the mixture for 15 seconds at a time, stirring after each interval. Continue until the mixture thickens to the consistency of dough. Let it cool down before using, as it will be too sticky when hot.

2. **Shaping the Coins**: Once the dough has cooled, have the children roll it into small balls and shape them into flat coins. You can also use small biscuit cutters to make them perfectly round. Don't flatten them too much, or they will break more easily once hard.
3. **Baking**: If you made the homemade clay, bake the coins at 175°F for 30-45 minutes. They're ready for painting once they've cooled completely. For modeling clay, simply shape the coins without baking, but they will need time to dry out (overnight works best).
4. **Painting**: After the coins have cooled or dried, let the children paint their coins with fun designs.
5. **Name the Coins:** Let the children name each coin for a talent they have.

My Notes:

Acknowledgements

Thank you to everyone who supported, encouraged, and prayed for me throughout the writing of this book. I am especially grateful to Marianne Linn, my faithful prayer partner for so many years, who has walked and prayed with me from the very beginning. I'm also thankful for the wonderful ladies in my small group at church—your prayers, enthusiasm, and genuine excitement continually spurred me forward.

This book exists because of the encouragement of so many. To my family and friends, your enthusiasm and care sustained me through every stage of this journey.

Thank you to my first readers who offered valuable feedback and edits – Crystal Oliveto, Heather Cook, Bob Schickler and Roxana Hudson.

My love and thanks go to my children—Rachel and Nick, Crystal and Matt, Brandon and Hannah, and Nicholas. You inspire me to press on in leaving a legacy. And to my grandchildren (and those yet to be born) who bring such joy to Grandkids Camp and make it all worthwhile: Nicholas, Joseph, Gwen, Dominic, Lennon, Kaden, Jackson and Benjamin and Aiden (our god-grandson). Hosting you at Grandkids Camp is one of our greatest joys.

A heartfelt thank you to my husband, Neal. Without your unwavering support, Grandkids Camp would not be possible. I love watching you with our grandchildren.

And above all, thanks be to God—without Him, none of this would be possible.

About Linda Quinones

Linda Quinones is the proud mother of four, grandmother of eight, and author of *Grandkids Camp: A Handbook for Leaving a Legacy Through Unforgettable Experiences Rooted in God's Word.* For over eight years, Linda and her husband, Neal, have hosted an annual "Grandkids Camp" at their lake home in Virginia—a cherished tradition that inspired her to share their camp plans, activities, and lessons learned so other grandparents can build meaningful memories and a lasting legacy of faith.

With over 40 years of experience working with children and program planning—through the YMCA, her church, her own business, and of course, raising her four children—Linda puts her heart into every camp experience with a wealth of creativity and insight.

You can connect with her at grandkidscampQ@gmail.com.

www.ingramcontent.com/pod-product-compliance
Lightning Source LLC
LaVergne TN
LVHW050614100826
845148LV00011B/1586

* 9 7 9 8 2 1 8 8 8 0 0 6 4 *